# Perfume Power

Joules Taylor, great-granddaughter of the herbalist and wisewoman of a small village in Devon, has enjoyed a lifelong interest in alternative lifestyles, conservation and health issues. A long-time user of organically grown and ecologically-sound products, she is conversant with most environmental issues and is currently researching scientific and political aspects of genetic modification. Joules has been writing on a wide-ranging variety of subjects for most of her life.

Other titles in the *Alternatives* series are:

*Astrology and Childhood* Peter West
*Coincidences: Towards a Greater Understanding* Tony Crisp
*Dreams and Dreaming: Understanding Your Sleep Messages* Tony Crisp
*Educate Your Memory: Memory Improvement for Students of All Ages* Billy Roberts
*Feng Shui Hour by Hour: Change Your Day* J. M. Sertori
*The Message of the Hands* Peter West
*Pen Pictures: Interpreting the Secrets of Handwriting* Peter West
*Personal Progress Through Positive Thinking* Hilary Jones and Frank Gilbert
*The Power of Peace: The Value of Meditation* Shirley Wallis
*Tarot for Today* Ken Taylor
*Visitation: The Certainty of Alien Activity* Peter Hough
*Working Memory: Improving Your Memory for the Workplace* Billy Roberts

# *Perfume Power*

**JOULES TAYLOR**

First published in Great Britain in 2000 by
LONDON HOUSE
114 New Cavendish Street
London W1M 7FD

Copyright © 2000 by Joules Taylor
The right of Joules Taylor to be identified as author of
this work has been asserted by her in accordance with the
Copyright, Designs and Patents Act, 1988

This book is sold subject to the condition that it shall not,
by way of trade or otherwise, be lent, resold, hired out
or otherwise circulated without the publisher's prior
written consent in any form of binding or cover other
than that in which it is published and without a
similar condition including this condition being imposed
upon the subsequent purchaser.

A catalogue record for this book is available
from the British Library

ISBN 1 902809 29 7

Edited and designed by DAG Publications Ltd, London.
Printed and bound by Biddles Limited,
Guildford, Surrey.

For more information about the author visit:
http://www.wordwrights.clara.net/contents.html

# *Acknowledgements*

With thanks to Jutta Blumenthal, M.H., Ir., for inspiration, to Carol Clutterbuck (Boots the Chemist) and Leianne Baxter (Guerlain at Bentalls) for their patience, information and advice. It was much appreciated!

*For Mum, with love.*

*For Carol, my Internet sister, for support and encouragment.*

*And for Ken, for still putting up with me after all this time!*

## Contents

Introduction: The Power of Perfume 9
1. The Sense of Smell a.k.a. 'The Science Bit …' 12
2. Perfumes for the Body and the Soul 18
3. Aromatherapy 30
4. Herbalism 54
5. Gardens 59
6. Feng Shui – a Fragrant Balance 80
7. Fragrant Foods 85
8. Perfumes 101
9. Crafty Perfumes! 111
10. Haunting Fragrances 123
Table of Essential Oils 132
A Cautionary Note 136
Notes 138
Bibliography 141
Index 143

# *Introduction*
# *The Power of Perfume*

Fragrance is all around us. It can enliven or soothe, arouse or nauseate. From the homely smell of fresh-baked bread, to the invigorating iodine and salt smell of the seashore; from the pungent sweat of a gymnasium changing room to the clinical, disinfectant smell of a hospital; from the sweet scents of a rose garden to the crisp, chill pine fragrance of a winter wood; there's no getting away from it – perfumes permeate our lives.[1]

The sense of smell is perhaps the least-regarded of all human senses, yet how powerful an effect it can have on our lives, our minds, even our bodies! As babies, we instinctively know the smell of our own mother and her milk. As we grow and develop, we begin to associate smells with places and occasions in our lives, both pleasant and unpleasant, and these create intimate, personal memories that stay with us forever. Sometimes it can be something very simple: the smell of butter sizzling in a pan always takes me back to a wonderful holiday in France, where the fresh vegetables for the daily *potage* (the French version of minestrone soup) were sautéed in butter every morning. Sometimes it can be more complicated: the faint, delicate fragrance of *Lunaria* flowers (commonly known as Honesty or Silver Dollar) is reminiscent – to me, at least – of the smell of quiet, sun-warmed, dusty attics, and reminds me irresistibly of my grandmother.

Try a small experiment. Close your eyes for a moment and think back to the most exciting holiday you ever took. Then remember the smells associated with it. These could be almost anything: the smoky smell of the log fire and the bouquet of glasses of brandy after a day on the *piste*; the indefinable aroma of the Mediterranean sun on Roman dust in the Colosseum; the innumerable spices of an Indian bazaar, or the smell of diesel oil, candyfloss and hot dogs at a seaside funfair. By imagining the smell, it's possible, for a moment, to feel yourself actually *there*, reliving the experience.

## INTRODUCTION

Our enjoyment of our food would be considerably lessened without the smells that go with it. Frying onions, pancakes with lemon juice or maple syrup, fresh strawberries, barbecued burgers, chocolate; the list is practically endless. On the other hand, where food is concerned our sense of smell can also serve to guard us against harm – generally speaking, foods that smell unpleasant are bad for us.[2] We also have individual dislikes which vary tremendously: the smell of prunes or boiling parsnips makes me feel nauseous, the first because even though I loathed the taste, I was forced to eat them at school as a small child; the second because I associate the smell with a nasty illness I suffered some years ago. The memories never fade …

Fragrance is important in relationships, both in the community and our intimate life. How someone smells when you first meet them will leave a lasting impression in your mind – and how you yourself smell will do the same for them. Most individuals prefer to be with people who smell 'clean' – the faint smell of soap, deodorant, mouthwash, light aftershave or cologne is both pleasant and implies consideration for the feelings – and noses – of others. (Bad breath and stale sweat is usually a big turn-off in any personal relationship – or in a crowded elevator, a check-out queue, or the workplace.) Most of us are familiar with the care and concern we take over our appearance and personal hygiene when preparing for an important meeting, whether romantic, personal or business, and we use fragrance almost without thinking as a part of that process. It makes us nicer to be with! (As long as we don't go too far. Heavy, cloying and overpowering scents stifle those all-important pheromones, and do *not* make a good impression …)

And perfumes can have a definite, beneficial effect on our physical bodies, both as stress-busters and to alleviate or cure a variety of ailments. We will consider aromatherapy, herbalism and various sorts of gardens later in the book, but for now I'll just mention the mixture of essential oils I employ, very successfully, when working. I use a deep-bowled fragrancer, half-filled with water, heated by a small candle: I add basil (for concentration), bergamot (to release tension), cedarwood (for depth of overall aroma, and because I really like the smell!), grapefruit (for stamina, vitality and enthusiasm), pine (eases aches and pains, and makes sitting at a desk for hours at a time less stressful) and a drop or two of rosemary (prevents headaches – for me, anyway). The number of drops of each oil is a matter of individual preference: I use far more of the grapefruit than the others, because I both need and appreciate its zingy, enlivening effect. By itself, however, although very pleasant, it doesn't have the same efficacy.

Most essential oils are very reasonably priced, and there are a great variety of vaporisers (fragrancers, perfume rings, humidifiers etc.) available. I would recommend experimenting with the perfumes[3] you find appealing: it is fun, often enlightening, generally good for you, and at the very least your home will smell wonderful!

Perfumes can be persuasive. How often have you been enticed into a shop because of the aroma of good coffee, baking bread, freesias, or new leather? And how often have you been able to resist buying something that smells so good, once you're in there? (Empty wallet aside, of course.) Even though we know that a lot of consumer outlets, realising the powerful allure of fragrance, now use it deliberately to draw in their customers, it still takes a great deal of will-power to resist. Scents of all kinds act upon a very fundamental part of ourselves, triggering all sorts of memories as well as responses we may not even consciously recognise. Understanding how and why we react as we do can open the way to a deeper enjoyment of life.

This book explores all aspects of fragrance, from how the sense of smell actually works, to making your own perfumes at home. Read it, use it, then go out and enjoy the rich, wonderfully aromatic world in which we live.

# 1
# *The Sense of Smell (a.k.a 'The Science Bit …')*

The brain is an extraordinary organ. About the size of a coconut, shaped like a walnut, and divided into lobes each dealing with particular functions or activities, the brain controls all body functions, processes internal and external stimuli, and is, essentially, responsible for who and what we are – in the conscious, rather than the genetically determined, sense.

The brain has grown and developed over time. The most ancient part, the 'reptilian brain' – the brainstem, right at the top of the spinal cord and so-called because it is similar to the entire brain of present-day reptiles – evolved more than 500 million years ago, and regulates the involuntary body functions (heart-beat, blood pressure, breathing). Above the brainstem is the limbic system (also called the 'mammalian brain', as it is believed to have first appeared in mammals), ancient, but still vitally important. The limbic system consists of several modules, which are densely and intimately connected to the more recently evolved parts of the brain. It is in this ancient part that emotions are generated (though not actually felt – that happens higher up in the frontal lobes), along with many of the basic urges that determine survival (fear, for example, which prompts the individual to take action – the well-known 'fight or flight' response – and also the sex drive). It is also the home of the hippocampus, which is essential for the laying down of long-term memory. Above the limbic system lies the cerebellum – our animal ancestor's main brain. At the top are the two hemispheres of the cerebrum, each with their four lobes. This is what most people envisage when they think of the human brain. The cerebrum is where most of the conscious activity of the brain takes place – visual and aural processing, thinking, planning, organising; it is also where most of our sense perception is centred. The sense of smell, however, is different.

## THE SENSE OF SMELL

How does the sense of smell actually work? Molecules of varying sizes are released from everything around us. They are breathed in automatically as we inhale, and as the nose fills with air, the molecules land on a small area of tissue, called the olfactory membrane, at the top of the nasal cavity. The membrane is filled with receptor cells – considered by many to be extensions of the brain itself – from which protrude thin hairs (cilia). Molecules[1] connect with the receptor cells, and the cilia register and transmit information about the smells (in the form of nerve impulses) to the olfactory bulb. This lies at the base of the brain, above the nasal cavity, on the other side of a thin section of the skull called the cribriform plate. From there, the impulses pass directly into the limbic system.

All the other senses affect the hemisphere *opposite* the side on which the stimulus is felt (images perceived with the right eye are processed on the left side of the brain and vice versa; sounds heard with the left ear are registered on the right hand side of the brain, etc.). In contrast, smells are processed on the same side of the brain as the nostril that perceives them.

That the initial processing of smells takes place within the limbic system goes quite some way towards explaining just why different aromas and odours have such a profound and powerful effect on us. The limbic system is the brain's emotional centre. Given the absolutely fundamental, albeit unconscious, functions of this part of our brain, it is not overly surprising that differing fragrances can affect our emotional or mental state, and even our physical body.

After this initial processing of the smell in the limbic system and the resultant emotional effect, the impulses travel to other parts of the brain – primarily the frontal and temporal lobes of the cerebrum – where the emotions they have generated are consciously recognised, analysed, enjoyed (or otherwise) and filed away in the memory.

For example: in an aromatherapy session, molecules of the essential oils which have been used travel directly to the olfactory membrane, where they attach themselves to the appropriate receptor cell. Information about the molecule is transmitted to the olfactory bulb, and from there to the limbic system, where the initial emotional response is generated (a state of relaxation, feeling of safety, happiness, simmering excitement, etc.). Electro-chemical impulses are then relayed to the frontal lobes and the appropriate neurochemicals are released to have their effect on the body – soothing, stimulating, euphoric etc. Of course, different impulses are transmitted to other parts of the body and brain, to register the actual physical effects of the essential oils – and tiny, aromatic particles of the oils also travel down into the lungs with the simple act of breathing.

It has also been found that certain molecules always gather in the same part of the human body, affecting that particular organ or tissue in the same way every time, thus allowing the discipline of aromatherapy to state with some confidence which oils are appropriate for which particular ailment or condition. Unfortunately, this does not just happen with beneficial molecules: Bristol University's study 'Children of the 90s' has found that volatile organic substances present in aerosol sprays – polish, air fresheners etc. – are toxic in concentration and can affect the body long after the spray has been used, leading to headaches and post-natal depression in new mothers as well as ear infections and stomach problems in their babies. It has also been discovered that chemical constituents of commercial perfumes and some sunscreen products can be absorbed into the skin and be passed to babies through their mother's milk. The human body is proving to be a far more subtle and responsive organism than was previously thought.

The human sense of smell is inferior to that of most animals. The sense of smell of dogs, who are probably the prime example of scent-sensitivity in the animal kingdom, is at least a million times more sensitive than that of humans. Dogs are able to recognise individual scents from a single flake of human skin (which, given that we lose on average tens of millions of skin cells every day, is pretty impressive). There has recently been other research carried out into dogs' sense of smell, and it appears that dogs are able to smell both the minute changes in body chemistry that signal an epileptic attack and the scent of malignant cells that are the first sign of cancer. There may come a time when dogs will be used to confirm the doctor's diagnosis – but of course far more research and experimentation needs to be conducted before we reach that stage.

It is not just members of the animal kingdom that have scent perception, however. Certain plants are able to sense the airborne chemical signature of harmful insects, at which they fill their leaves full of toxins to deter the bugs. Moreover, if the danger persists the plant can continue to produce poisons until it collapses and dies. (A kind of vegetable 'death before dishonour'?)

Humans, of course, have developed other ways of alerting themselves to danger and acquiring those things needed for continued existence, and our once quite highly developed sense of smell is now generally underused – consciously at least.

There is, however, a way to improve our scent perception: simply concentrate on becoming more aware of the smells around you. Breathe deeply and try identifying the aromas you notice. Avoid smoky or polluted atmospheres if you can, and spend more time in the countryside or in gardens. See if you can identify friends and relatives by their scent! Learning to appreciate the world through your nose opens up a host of new experiences.

In a primitive world, the senses of sight, smell and hearing are by far the most important for survival (catching food, finding a mate, and avoiding danger). It is not too surprising that all three figured very largely in the evolution of the limbic system to the extent that a specific module, the thalamus, developed to allow all three senses to operate together smoothly. The thalamus also forwards incoming information to the correct areas of the brain for further processing.

In humans the nasal cavity is also the site of two strange little pits, halfway up each nostril. These were first identified by a Danish anatomist, Jacobsen, in 1811, and have been called Jacobsen's Organ ever since. They appear to be receptors for especially heavy scent molecules, and they lead directly into the limbic system. It has been proposed, and is generally accepted, that they are the site of our sensitivity towards pheromones.

Pheromones, according to the dictionary, are chemical substances secreted by animals which affect the behaviour or physiology of other animals of the same species. In humans, pheromones are present in sweat and genital fluids, and play a large part in determining whether we find an individual attractive or not. Pheromones are essentially odourless – in any event, we are not consciously aware of them – but, they pass into the hypothalamus, part of the limbic system, which then stimulates the sexual response, one of the most powerful in the entire human organism. (So the next time you find yourself drawn to exactly the wrong type of person, blame the pheromones!)

## Psychological Effects

The human body was once viewed as a machine – intricate, but explicable in terms of other machines. These days, the incredible complexity of the human organism is better known, though still not complete, and the close and complicated relationship between our health and our emotional state is widely recognised. Having seen how profoundly the sense of smell can affect us, mentally, emotionally and physically, it is not too surprising to hear that smell also plays a significant role in the fairly new discipline of psychoneuroimmunology. This studies the way in which thought influences the processes of the brain. Most people are probably aware that certain areas can be stimulated by consciously recreating mental states, for example, thinking about something really distressing can induce all the symptoms of deep grief, even when there is literally nothing to cry about. (This is, of course, something that marks the good actor from the simply competent. Being able to portray intense emotional states without actually experiencing them physically is a wonderful skill.)

By influencing the brain, conscious thought can also influence an individual's whole outlook on life, and thus how they react to illness.

Psychoneuroimmunology proposes that an unhappy mental state lowers the human resistance to illness, effectively reducing the efficiency of the immune system. Conversely, a happy and positive mental state improves our health and our ability to heal quickly. This may seem like old news to the large number of people who already believe that positive thinking is the best cure for just about any ailment. It is nice to know that scientists are catching up!

It is known that the neural pathways that make the whole process actually work do exist, but identifying how they operate is less easy because different people react differently to the same stimulus. Some interesting experiments have been carried out with groups of volunteers testing pain-killing drugs. Often, the group given the placebo (dummy) pain-killers respond better than those given the real thing – the *belief* that the drug will work being stronger and more effective than its actual constituents! The new discipline is gradually making its way onto the medical college syllabus, so it is to be hoped that a better understanding of the process will soon be forthcoming.

Of course, having scientific proof of a particular idea usually makes it a viable subject for commercial use (or possible abuse), and the notion that fragrance can influence mood and even job performance was speedily picked up and exploited. After all, it is not difficult to introduce a little aromatherapy into the workplace: simply add essential oils to the air conditioning system. Some gymnasiums have started using the aroma of peppermint in their changing rooms: it is stimulating and tonic, and can improve performance in the gym and on the sportsfield (as well as helping combat the smell of sweat). It has been suggested that office workers may benefit from fragrances that will keep them alert but soothed at the same time – apparently, in Los Angeles, casinos and other gambling emporiums are experimenting with blends that will make their 'guests' feel optimistic! Japan already employs aromas to help its salarymen and other office employees stay sharp-witted right the way through the long working day.

With the exception of the gamblers, these may be considered reasonably sensitive and positive uses of the power of fragrances. Ethical problems arise, however, when suggestions of pumping calming aromas through schools in order to help teachers maintain control over ebullient or disruptive children are mooted. It would be relatively easy to flood prisons with sedative aromas, as well. Of course, such controlling measures would affect the teachers and wardens too, unless they took steps to avoid breathing in the fragrances. (Masks, perhaps? Not such a good idea in schools …)

The difficulty is deciding where to draw the line, not something the human race has shown itself to be particularly competent at doing. However, given the profound effect our sense of smell has on our physical, mental and emotional well-being, it may be time to start discussing legislation – or at the very least some sort of ethical code.

# 2
# Perfumes for the Body and the Soul

Given the profound effect fragrance has on our body and mind, it is hardly surprising that since time immemorial perfumes have been associated with the gods, the soul and spiritual qualities.

From the very earliest graves, with their simple floral offerings, through Egyptian mummification procedures and the burning incense that carried prayers to the gods, to the great floral displays in churches, plants and their essential essences have played a major role in religious practices for millennia.

## The Egyptians

Egypt boasts an immensely ancient heritage: tools at least half a million years old have been discovered there, and it is likely that the cattle were first domesticated about eleven thousand years ago. Certainly villages were in existence to the east of the Nile delta around six thousand years ago. Generally speaking, however, our knowledge of Egyptian civilisation starts with the Old Kingdom, which lasted from 2625–2130 BCE.

Egypt relied on the annual flooding of the Nile for its prosperity. Although the flood could vary dramatically (and in some instances catastrophically, if it was too high, too low or receded too quickly) in a good year the floods lasted from mid-June to mid-October, and crops planted as the flood waters receded were ready for harvest from February until just before the next year's flood. A wide range of foodstuffs was grown – wheat, barley, pulses, garlic, lettuce, cucumber, onions, leeks and radishes, while orchards provided pomegranates, melons, figs, dates and grapes (used for making both red and white wines). Flax, sesame seeds and the castor-oil plant provided oils, and numerous herbs were grown for medicinal purposes, including rosemary, basil, cumin, dill, mint and juniper berries. Spices included fenugreek,

## PERFUMES FOR THE BODY AND THE SOUL

coriander, saffron, cardamom, caraway, cassia and henna (used, as it still is today, as a dye for the hair, and also for the nails of mummies). Acacia, the myrrh bush (*Commiphora myrrha*), balm of Gilead (*Commiphora gileadensis*), horseradish tree (*Moringa peregrina* – the ben oil extracted from the seeds was extensively used in cooking and cosmetics), Egyptian plum (*Balanites aegyptica*), and the frankincense tree (*Boswellia sp*.) were also used for timber, oil and resin. Cypress and cedarwood were imported for use in medicine and building.

But throughout the ages, the Egyptians also appreciated their flowers, as shown by their decorative arts and the wreaths and floral tributes that accompanied the dead on their journey into the afterlife. Taking probably the best known archaeological find – the tomb treasures of the boy-king Tutankhamun – as an example, wreaths and necklaces of cornflowers, willow, celery and olive leaves, chamomile flowers (sacred to the sun god Re), and blue lotus waterlilies were found in the sarcophagus and decorating the king's personal possessions. Although papyrus, palms and the lotus waterlily figured heavily in Egyptian decoration, poppies and mandrakes are also found. Madonna lilies were cultivated for their perfume, while safflower was grown as a dye for cloth.

Egyptians placed a great deal of importance on the sense of smell. During the Early Dynastic Period (3000 BCE onwards) the craft of perfumery was already well-developed, and the priesthood allocated different perfumes to different gods in the Egyptian pantheon. Such perfumes were used to anoint statues of the deities or poured as libations when asking for aid. It does not take a great stretch of the imagination to think of the perfume being able to impart the skills and attributes of the god to a person wearing the same fragrance,[1] although it is extremely unlikely that anyone but the highest ranking personage would be permitted such an honour. However, we can imagine the Pharaoh anointing himself with the perfumes of Hathor, Toth, Ma'at or Osiris, depending on whether he was engaged in rituals of love, learning, justice or salvation.

Incense was also burned in temples, both on altars and in censers, the prayers of the priests symbolically ascending with the fragrant smoke exactly as they do today in faiths which use incense as part of their religious rites. The burning of fragrant (or sometimes not so fragrant!) materials to represent supplications, questions or appeals from man to his gods is an ancient, venerable and well-nigh indestructible facet of worship.

That Egyptians regarded the use of perfume as a necessary part of personal hygiene is clear – wax cones worn on the heads of guests and musicians at banquets and official occasions melted in the heat, releasing a strong fragrance that would have sweetened the air, while the earliest recorded recipe for a deodorant dates to 1500 BCE![2] Numerous tomb paintings depict the deceased smelling a lotus flower, a charming symbol for rejuvenation after death. (The lotus, like the daisy, opens in the morning light, closes its petals at night, and opens again the following day, making it a visual representation of rebirth for the Egyptians, who believed in an afterlife very similar to the life they had led on earth.)

It was vitally important that the bodies of the dead be preserved as scrupulously as possible in order for the deceased to enjoy the afterlife to the full. Initially this was accomplished by burying the deceased in shallow pits in the desert – the sand and heat naturally desiccated the bodies (assuming, of course, that scavengers such as jackals did not get to them first. It is likely, incidentally, that the god of mummification – Anubis – came to be regarded as a jackal or jackal-headed human figure as a talismanic means of transmuting the graveyard-haunting jackal from a despoiler of the dead to the protector of the deceased, a little like employing the poacher as a gamekeeper.) While similar relatively simple forms of burial would have continued for the poor, it was not long before the rich felt it necessary for much more elaborate funerary rites. The status and condition of the individual in the afterlife depended primarily upon the circumstances of his or her burial. They took their possessions with them or, if this was not possible, a model of the possession was buried instead. Even the poor were buried with 'soul houses', little models of the house in which they lived while alive and hoped to inhabit in the afterlife. But most important was the body.

The process of mummification became more elaborate over time. In pre-dynastic times (until 3000 BCE), the body was wrapped in resin-soaked linen bandages and placed in wood- or brick-lined tombs. By the time of the Fourth Dynasty (2625–2500 BCE) chemical mummification using natron – a compound of sodium carbonate and bicarbonate – was employed and continued for the next three thousand years. However, oils and resins were still used to preserve the body tissues and doubtless to perfume the corpse, making it more acceptable both to itself and to its judges in the afterlife.

Cedarwood oil, from imported cedar of Lebanon, was known to have antiseptic qualities, and would have been one of the most useful preservatives. Frankincense, and more particularly myrrh, juniper berries and basil oil, were also utilised in the process, and the mummified body was often interred in an aromatic cypress wood coffin. Incense of myrrh and juniper would have accompanied prayers for the safe journey of the deceased through the halls of judgement and his or her attainment of bliss in the afterlife. An Egyptian funeral must have been a very fragrant affair!

## Middle East

Babylon – the city whose name is still used today to denote luxury, richness and a slightly decadent extravagance – was one of the principal towns of another very ancient culture, the Assyro-Babylonian civilisation. Babylon was also the source of the Code of Hammurabi, established around 1800 BCE, a set of laws aiming to unify Babylonian legal practices that also had an interesting code of punishment for unsuccessful surgeons: if a patient was harmed by a surgeon (for example, if he lost an eye) the surgeon paid the same penalty (his own eye was removed). The USA was not the first country to indulge in medical litigation! Babylonian warriors were known to have combed perfumed oil through their hair.

This culture, which comprised two neighbouring peoples, the Akkadians and the Sumerians, flourished from around 3000 BCE. As with most ancient peoples, a pantheon of deities was worshipped – often varying slightly from town to town – and incense was most often used to ensure that prayers addressed to the gods actually reached them.

*The Epic of Gilgamesh*[3] has numerous references to the use of fragrances – oils, woods etc. – throughout its length, and most particularly where prayers of sacrifice are offered to the gods.

Before he sets out on his quest, Gilgamesh's mother offers prayers for his safety:

> Ninsun[4] climbed to the roof, and there she prepared a censer to Shamash.[5]
> Lifting her arms, scattering incense, she appealed to the Sun God:
> 'Why did you afflict my son with such a restless, wandering spirit? ...
> If it must be so, then guard him well ...'

Further in the Epic is an account of the Deluge,[6] spoken by Utnapishtim,[7] the survivor of the flood. When the raven he had released from his boat found dry land and did not return, he landed on a mountaintop and prepared a thanksgiving offering:

> 'I flung everything open to the four winds in exultation:
> I made sacrifice, burned incense, poured a libation,
> Fourteen vessels I set in position, reed, cedar and myrtle I piled beneath them.
>
> 'And the gods took notice of the sweet smell of my sacrifice –
> The gods gathered like flies ...'

But fragrance was used for more mundane – if no less important – purposes as well ...

> Lady Ishtar[8] looked with yearning on the beauty of Gilgamesh.
> 'Come beloved, be my bridegroom!
> Grant me your fruits, O grant me!
> Be my husband and let me be your wife!
>
> 'Let me harness a chariot of lapis lazuli and gold,
> With wheels of gold and trappings of amber.
> Driving lions in a team, yoked with mules of great size,
> Enter our home, filled with the sweet smell of cedar!'

Durable, sweet-scented and insect-repellent, cedar wood – most often from the cedar of Lebanon, until over-felling of the tree made it comparatively rare – has been used extensively in the Middle East throughout the centuries, both in building and for export: the fragrant wood can be burned as an incense. It has even found its way to the New World – old Bermudan cedarwood furniture retains its rich, warm fragrance for hundreds of years, and is much sought after. The tall, stately and very long-lived tree has been used as a metaphor for the righteous:

> They shall flourish like the fruitful palm, grow steadily like the cedar in Lebanon.[9]

and as the dwelling of kings. So many cedars were cut down to line the stone-built Temple of Jerusalem and the Palace of Solomon, that deforestation was the main contributory factor to the area becoming desert. There is also a tradition that God told King Solomon to make the Temple's furniture from sandalwood, which would have been imported from further east. Between the warm, dark fragrance of cedarwood and the sweet perfume of sandalwood the Temple would have smelled truly heavenly!

One of the most famous – and beautiful – examples of the use of fragrance to express sensuality and depth of emotion is the Song of Songs. This outpouring of love and desire is filled with aromatic imagery:

> While the king sat at his banquet
> My spikenard[10] sent forth its fragrance.
> My beloved is to me as a bundle of myrrh
> That lies between my breasts ...

(Ch 1, lines 12-13)

> ... our couch is moss and grass,
> The beams of our house are cedar,
> And the rafters are fir ...

(Ch 1, lines 16-17)

> Who is this that comes up out of the wilderness like a pillar of smoke,
> Perfumed with myrrh and frankincense,
> With all the spices the merchants can bring?

(Ch 3, line 6)

> The fragrance of your clothes is like the perfume of Lebanon.
> As a private garden are you, my bride,
> A dammed spring, a secret fountain;
> Your shoots are an orchard of pomegranates, an abundance of precious fruits,
> Henna and spikenard plants,
> Spikenard and saffron, calamus[11] and cinnamon,
> With all trees of frankincense
> Myrrh and aloes and all the most costly spices.

(Ch 4, lines 11-14)

The resins – principally frankincense – that provided the main constituents of incense for Hebrew religious purposes also played a considerable role in life in general. They were utilised in making perfumes and for cleansing the air, particularly in sickrooms. They were costly, of course, and not available to all. In religious rites, incense was burned as a sacrifice (or added to a sacrifice: the scent of burning frankincense would help to disguise the odour of charring flesh), to provide – literally – a fragrant smokescreen for the presence of a god whose glory might otherwise strike the priest dead, or as a means of driving away demons.

Over time, frankincense began to be seen as symbolic of godhood. There is a tale in Marco Polo's *The Travels* which clarifies the Biblical story of the visit of the Three Wise Men to the newborn Jesus:

> In Persia there is a city called Saveh, and three days further on is a town called Kala Atashparastan ... The people there say that in ancient times three kings of Persia went to give

reverence to a newly born prophet, taking with them offerings of gold, frankincense and myrrh. They said amongst themselves: 'If he accepts the gold, he is an earthly king; if frankincense, a god; if myrrh, a healer of men.' But the child took all three offerings, and the kings decided that he was at once a god, an earthly king, **and** a healer ...[12]

For some centuries after the destruction of the Temple – around 70 CE – incense dropped out of use. It began to be used again in the fifth century, firstly to show respect for venerable and respected people, and later to represent prayers addressed to the deity, which to a large extent remains its function today.

Historically and traditionally, Arabia was the source of fabulous treasures and luxury goods, not just the rose orchards from which came the rose essential oil that supplied the civilised world for so long. Other fragrant products included flower waters (rose and musk, orange-flower, lily, violet) incense (ambergris and musk) and floral perfumes (rose, violet, myrtle and anemone). Perfumed breath, especially if scented with ambergris, was considered seductive and romantic. Indeed, a fragrant atmosphere was considered so desirable that the mortar used in the building of mosques was also perfumed with oils. This was an art learned, it would appear, from the Babylonians, who used the same method in the construction of their temples, but used cedarwood, myrrh and cypress oils which would be more intense when warmed by the sun, so that the faithful could worship encircled by a faint but unmistakable fragrance.

## The Classical World

In ancient Greece, sweet fragrances were accorded a divine origin, both gifts from and symbols of the gods. In Elysium, the Greek heaven, perfumed rivers scented the air with a rich, sweet aroma.

As in most cultures, the rose – the flower of Aphrodite and Venus (respectively the Greek and Roman goddesses of love) – was regarded as the supreme flower by the civilisations of Ancient Greece and Rome. In Greece, rose oil was used to anoint the dead, as well as being offered, in beautiful and costly vessels, as sacrifices to the gods and in particular to Aphrodite. But roses were used by the living, too: the Greeks drew the perfume from the petals with salt, coloured the resultant liquid a delicate pink, and used it to anoint themselves. In the fourth century BCE, Theophrastus, a noted Greek botanist, advised mixing rose perfume with sesame oil to make the perfume last longer. Interestingly, he suggested that rose perfume was inappropriate for women's use – because of its subtlety!

The ancient Greeks also used basil and fennel for cosmetic purposes, and Greeks and Romans burned lavender to ward off disease. Thyme and rosemary were both burned as incense in temples.

The Romans rather went to town in their use of roses. Nets full of rose petals were suspended above the heads of guests at banquets and released at the appropriate times, the boxes used for noble spectators at the public games were wreathed with thousands of the blooms, and temples and shrines were festooned with them. At one point, a considerable amount of arable land was given over to the growing of roses; the crop proved much more profitable than food staples.

In personal life, too, roses figured largely in Roman society. Rose oil, like the variety of quartz crystal known as amethyst, was reputed to counteract the intoxicating effect of too much wine, and vast quantities were used to anoint the heads of diners at feasts. Wealthy Romans bathed in rose water, and afterwards had themselves massaged with rose-scented lotions. Noble Romans must have smelled rather overwhelmingly of a rose garden!

**The East**
In Japan, aromatic cypress wood was used to build graceful, elegant temples and shrines, while in India, the earliest temples were constructed of sandalwood. (A little different from the wattle-and-daub – woven hazel twigs daubed with a mix of clay and cow-dung – which went into the construction of early European dwellings!)

Incense has always played a large part in religious observances in the east. In Japan, the sweet smoke is believed to transport the prayers of the living to the souls of the ancestors, while in India the fragrant clouds honour the deities as the appeals and worship of the devotees ascend.

The Indian joss stick – a pencil-thin, slow-burning incense moulded around a stick – is formed from plant oils mixed, traditionally, with mud from the sacred Ganges. The sticks should be inserted into a holder (there are many sorts available, from ski-shaped wooden dishes to eggcup-shaped brass vessels), lit, and left to burn. The smoke has a dark, earthy aroma underlying the sweeter fragrance, making it ideal for meditation on things of the body.

Sandalwood, in particular, has a special place in Ayurvedic medicine for its superior healing properties. It is also reputed to improve the memory. That perfume was generally available to the ordinary people is shown in the *Ramayana* (from 2000 BCE), where perfumers and incense sellers, as well as weavers, lamp-makers and millers, were amongst the people who came into the streets to welcome home the hero, Rama of Ayodhya.

### America

That the burning of herbs for religious or ritual purposes is very much a global phenomenon is shown by the ancient Amerindian practice of 'smudging'. Like the burning of incense, smudging is a method of purifying or sanctifying a sacred space. The herbs are burned – smouldered, actually – to release their fragrance and subtle energy.

Smudging (occasionally called smoking, although the herbs are not inhaled as though from a cigarette) can take two different forms. Perhaps the best known is the smudge stick – a bundle of herbs braided together, or simply tied as a bunch, and allowed to dry naturally. The end of the bundle or braid is applied to fire – either a candle flame or a hearthfire (it can take a minute or two for the bundle to start smouldering correctly, so matches are usually not used) and allowed to smoke during the ritual. The other method is to crumble the dried herbs and burn a pinch or two on a fire or charcoal block – this way gives the user more control over the amount of smoke produced, and is perhaps more appropriate for modern buildings. It is important, of course, to ensure that the container used for the heat source is fireproof, and that any burning or smoking material is not left unattended.

A number of different herbs are used, each with their own significance and purpose. Lavender, with its soothing, healing abilities, is used for emotional cleansing, and is employed in combination with other herbs for different purposes. With rosemary, it can assist the mind to relax during regression sessions as well as improve the memory in two ways: the capacity for remembering more clearly and effectively in the future and the remembrance of things long past. Combined with cedar, one of the traditional smudging materials, it is helpful for achieving and maintaining an even keel in your life and assisting in balancing your emotional needs. With thyme, it can aid the acceptance of the physical for those who may live too much in their own fantasy worlds, or have developed their mental abilities at the expense of the body – the combination of lavender and thyme can act as a powerful 'grounding' agent.

The traditional herbs of sweetgrass, white sage and cedar are mostly used for spiritual purposes, to purify the one using the bundle or burner. The smoke is fanned towards the body, clearing out unhealthy and negative energy and replacing it with positive and healing powers. Traditionally, the rising smoke was also a means of communication between the earthly folk and their spirit helpers – effectively carrying prayers and requests to the unseen world, much as incense does the world over.

## Northern Europe

Fragrance has always held a unique place in the hearts of European people, partly because so much of the continent is too cold to be able to produce the sort of gloriously perfumed plants that inhabit warmer climes. Nevertheless, many of the native aromatic plants became linked to particular deities. Violets and pine, for example, symbolise Cernunnos (Herne), the Lord of the Animals and of growing things as well as the Great Goddess's son and consort, and an incense using these plants may be burned during his rites (for example at Yule, when he is born, or at Samhain, when he symbolically dies). Primrose, cowslip and narcissus are special to Eostre, the representation of the Great Goddess as the deity of springtime fertility. The fabled Tir N'an Og – the Summerlands, to which the souls of the dead travel for rest and relaxation before being reincarnated on earth – is filled with the sweet scents of summer, especially the delicate scent of apple blossom, one of the most wonderful of all Northern European natural fragrances.

The legendary Holy Grail, reputedly the cup that held the wine Christ served to his disciples at the Last Supper, has held a place in the imagination since the early thirteenth century. There is a further legend that the Grail also caught Christ's blood at the Crucifixion, making it doubly blessed. This most elusive and mysterious of mystical icons has a fragrance as though 'all the costliest spices of the world flowed therefrom'. The Holy Grail is reputed to restore the dead to life – the land and the soul, as well as the body.[13] There is something very satisfying in the equation of the miraculous and the gloriously fragrant ...

**Floral Tributes**
The living, as well as the dead, have been honoured with fragrant, floral tributes since time immemorial. A gift of flowers seems to be the first thing everyone thinks of to commemorate a special occasion. The list is extensive: fragrant flowers for the new mother; red roses for the special girlfriend (or boyfriend – let's be equitable!), fiancée or spouse to celebrate a birthday or anniversary; a posy of primroses or violets for Mother's Day; fragrant garlands to greet visitors in places such as Hawaii, Sri Lanka and India; wedding bouquets and posies; and the funeral wreath or tribute. Then there are the floral representatives of the seasons – the pot of hyacinths for the spring, roses or honeysuckle for the summer, fruits and dried leaves for the autumn, and mistletoe, holly and poinsettia for the winter.

# 3
# *Aromatherapy*

**Introduction**

The word 'aromatherapy' was coined by René-Maurice Gattefossé in the early 20th century to describe the therapeutic use of the essential oils that produce a plant's actual aroma, but the use of plants for medicinal purposes goes back tens of thousands of years. Initially, and for millennia, herbalism[1] – the use of various parts of specific plants to treat physical ailments – was the *only* medicine (apart from magic) available to the human race. We cannot know for certain when the first essential oils were extracted from plants, but the first liquid perfumes – most probably flower waters – were already being prepared for use as long ago as 3500 BCE, so it is not unreasonable to assume that methods for obtaining the oils were developed soon after. Certainly it is believed that the earliest methods of distillation were practised in India, ancient Persia and Egypt thousands of years ago. In India plants and plant extracts have been used medically for at least 5,000 years.

In Egypt during the Early Dynastic Period – from 3000 BCE onwards – the craft of perfumery was already well developed, and the priesthood allocated different perfumes to different gods in the Egyptian pantheon. This procedure was echoed by Nicholas Culpeper in Britain in the early 17th century. His *Complete Herbal* allocates each herb to a different astrological planet, themselves named after the gods of Rome and partaking, astrologically speaking, of the virtues and potency of the deities involved.[2]

But even the common people had access to some fragrances. Herbs and aromatic woods were burned to sweeten the air, incidentally helping to destroy the spread of air-borne bacteria and thus maintain a healthier population. Cones of scented wax were worn on the head, particularly on special occasions: in the heat the wax melted and dripped down the body, helping to deter insects and keep the individual pleasant to be with. And the earliest (1500 BCE) recorded recipe for a deodorant can be found in the Egyptian *Papyrus Ebers*. The Egyptians took their personal hygiene seriously, but then, so did most ancient peoples.[3] Most of us are familiar with the great communal baths of Rome, but there are other examples found around the world: one, discovered by archaeologists in a city in what is now Pakistan, dates back to around 5000 BCE.

Throughout the ancient world knowledge of the use of plants and their extracts spread and developed, becoming adapted for local use depending on what was available either as native plants or imported goods. The Romans learned from the Egyptians and Greeks, and took seeds with them on their voyages of conquest. Those traditionally most British of all herbs – parsley, sage, rosemary and thyme – are actually not native at all, but naturalised Mediterranean plants grown from seed brought over by the Roman legions. Herbs and spices from the Orient and the Spice Islands[4] – ginger, cloves, pepper, cardamom, cinnamon – were transported along the Silk Road, sometimes taking years to reach their destination and therefore rare, precious and incredibly expensive. Persia became the provider of rose oil to the rest of the known world. And at the end of the 9th century CE, a Persian by the name of Ibn Sina (better known to us as Avicenna) revolutionised the distillation apparatus used in extracting the oils, making the process both faster and more efficient,[5] and thus correspondingly less expensive and more plentiful. Essential oils were now within the reach of far more people than before.

Over the next thousand years, aromatic plants and herbs were cultivated in monasteries, used in attempts to combat plagues, and their therapeutic and medicinal qualities investigated and refined. It was not really until the end of the 19th century that what most people understand as 'science' stepped in, and began to isolate and synthesise their active therapeutic properties in the laboratory. However, these powerful synthetic drugs frequently have unpleasant, if not serious, side effects, and the early years of the 20th century saw a resurgence of interest in natural medicine – certainly for those irritating but non-serious little aches and ailments from which we all suffer, although aromatherapy and other complementary therapies have been shown to have a place in the treatment of more serious illness, too.

Although it was already in use in France as a gentle, alternative medicine, aromatherapy was first introduced into the UK in the late 1950s not by the medical profession, but as a beauty procedure – therapeutic massage. Essential oils (in a suitable carrier) take between 30 minutes to 12 hours to be absorbed into the skin, and the massage techniques were utilised to relieve stress and ease minor skin conditions. In those days, the actual constituents of the blends used for massage were kept a secret: now, of course, it is possible to buy almost any essential oil and carrier, and books on massage techniques, and other uses for the oils, are readily available so everyone can try it out for themselves. From inhaling the steam from a basin of eucalyptus oil in boiling water to help clear blocked sinuses, to pampering tired, swollen, neglected feet in a basin of warm water with a drop or two of peppermint, lavender and geranium, essential oils are a natural, safe[6] and effective way of improving our quality of life at minimal cost to ourselves or our world.

## The Art and Science of Aromatherapy

Aromatherapy is the therapeutic use of essential oils – natural plant essences that have been extracted by a recognised method (see below, Extraction Methods). These essences are stored in specialised cells or reservoirs in different parts of different plants, and extracted from those parts: rose and neroli (orange blossom), for example, from the petals; geranium from the leaves and stalks; pine from the pine needles (from *Pinus sylvestris* to be exact); the citruses (lemon, grapefruit, bergamot etc.) from the peel of the fruits; sandalwood and cedarwood from, of course, the wood; ginger and carrot from the roots; juniper from the berries; frankincense and myrrh from the resin of their trees. The amount of essence that each type of plant produces varies tremendously, from the abundant oils of the citrus fruits and lavender to the minute amount that can be distilled from rose petals (something like one ounce of oil to 60,000 roses[7]) – the price varies accordingly! Generally speaking, as long as we buy from a reputable[8] source, the quality of the oil is reflected in the price we pay.

Whether you intend using them medicinally or simply to experiment with fragrances for the home, in the bath or as gifts, buy the purest oils you can find. As a general rule of thumb, oils bought from a health food store are likely to be more 'authentic' than those bought from a perfumery outlet or chemist. Financially speaking, it makes sense to buy the real thing: much less is needed to be effective than if you use adulterated or synthetic oils.

Despite the name, most essential oils are not actually oily. They are, however, very complex liquids, containing a hundred or more different chemical components. Some of these have not yet been identified, and others appear to have no readily apparent purpose (although they may act to reduce the irritating effect of some of the active constituents in certain oils). In synthetic oils, many of these components are missing, reducing the quality – and possibly leading to undesirable side effects, as many synthetic drugs have done. Essential oils can fulfil all the requirements we expect of modern drugs, but in a much gentler, safer way. They do not, as far as we presently know, remain in the body (unlike chemical drugs), and except for rare cases of skin sensitivity, have no side effects.

Professional aromatherapists – indeed, many practitioners of complementary medicine – believe that all living things (and, sometimes, inorganic material such as crystals) contain an invisible and unquantifiable 'life force'. In human beings this would be called the soul or spirit. Although the human body can be likened to a complex biochemical machine, and even the mind can be understood as the result of genetics, upbringing, and our responses to external stimuli, humans are far more than the sum of their parts. There is something, unique to each of us, that makes us who (not what) we are. Cynics, and those who refuse to believe in anything that can not be scientifically proven, will deny it – a dubious attitude, since yesterday's magic and superstition is tomorrow's science – but most of us are conscious of some vital spark within. It is this life force in the plant kingdom which gives essential oils their subtle but extremely potent energy. It's missing from synthetic oils, which is another reason to avoid using them.

## Extraction Methods

**Steam distillation** is the most popular and economical method. It is an art in itself, especially when preparing low-yield plants such as roses for processing, but the basic method is straightforward. The plant material – leaves and flowers, crushed seeds or stalks, grated woods – is placed in a still and heated steam passed through it from the bottom. The tiny molecules of the essential oil evaporate into the steam, which is then cooled, and the resultant liquid collected. The oil separates from the water (they have different densities) and is drawn off and bottled. The water contains a very small amount of some of the oil's components, along with some of the larger, water-soluble plant molecules, and has something of the fragrance of the original plant. This is known as an aromatic water and is marketed as such (lavender water, for example).

With expensive, low-yield plants like rose, a method called 'cohobation' (using the same water over and over again until it becomes saturated with every last molecule of the oil, which is then condensed out) ensures that nothing is lost. Inexpensive commercially available 'rose water' is invariably synthetic.

Two recent variations on steam distillation are carbon dioxide extraction and hydrodiffusion. The former uses compressed carbon dioxide – at very high pressures and very low temperatures – and requires specialised and expensive equipment; it is claimed that the oils extracted by this method are closer to those in the original plant (and therefore 'purer') than others. Hydrodiffusion works along the same lines as a coffee percolator: steam is forced through the plant material from the top, the resultant oil and condensed steam collected at the bottom, and cooled and separated as in steam distillation. The process is the quickest (and therefore most efficient) of the distillation methods currently being used, and the oils produced seem to be particularly rich and intense.

**Expression** is only used to extract the oils from citrus fruits. Anyone who has ever peeled an orange will know how easy it is to express these oils, which stud the fruit just under the surface of the rind and spray out (in my case usually into my face!) under pressure. To profit from the whole fruit, factories processing citrus fruit for their juices often express oils as well, so care should be taken when choosing or using these oils: unless they are subsequently distilled, pesticide residues may be present. Orange oil from the USA, where oranges are big business and pesticide and fertiliser use is widespread, is probably the least dependable.

**Solvent extraction** employs solvents (hydrocarbons such as benzene, for example, or alcohol) to extract absolutes and resinoids from the raw materials. Resinoids are produced from tree resins while absolutes come from plants. They are primarily used by the perfume industry, not the aromatherapist, since they are not classified as essential oils. Commercially available jasmine is an absolute, rather than an oil, but has such a wonderful fragrance and is so well loved that not mentioning it would be a crime!

**Maceration** involves chopping up the plant material, adding it to a container of warm oil (almond or sunflower), agitating for several days, then filtering out the plant material. Essential oils – as well as other plant constituents – are soluble in vegetable oil, so this method is sometimes used to reap the benefits of the essence of plants which are too expensive or difficult to be processed in any other way. It is a method that can be tried at home: half fill a jar with your chosen plant, add warmed vegetable oil, and leave in a warm place for a week, shaking occasionally. Filter to remove the leaves etc., and bottle for use as a massage oil or, indeed, as a food flavouring if you opted for one of the traditional kitchen garden herbs.

**Enfleurage**, an ancient method, involves laying leaves or petals on cold animal fat and replacing them regularly until the plant extracts have saturated the fat. The fat and plant material mix can also be pressed between layers of glass to speed up the process.

## Carriers

Carriers are not necessarily oils, although most people automatically think of oils when the subject is mentioned. In fact, a carrier is any medium which carries the essential oil into the body. Air is the carrier for essential oils used in a fragrancer – the best method to employ if you are using the oils to perfume a room or to combat airborne viruses, as several of the oils are known to do – or sniffed from a tissue; water if they are being used in the bath; and carrier oils when the essential oils are being diluted for application directly onto the skin.

There are quite a variety of carrier oils available, all with their own properties and sold at widely varying prices. If you feel inclined to experiment with aromatherapy massage techniques, you could consider using sweet almond oil. It is perhaps the best known (and very often the least expensive): it protects and soothes the skin, making it appropriate for most people. Evening primrose oil is beneficial for dry skin – it has the reputation of caring for and improving the condition of wrinkled, ageing skin, too – and is quite reasonably priced, although using it to treat large areas of skin could end up being very expensive. It should be diluted with another carrier oil before use; 10% evening primrose oil to 90% other oil is usually recommended. Cold-pressed sunflower oil is helpful in treating ulcers and skin diseases, and has diuretic properties.

Tiny quantities of essential oils are absorbed into the skin during massage, and carried throughout the body by the bloodstream – another reason to ensure that the oils you use are as pure as possible. A professional aromatherapist will take into account your age, weight, general health and, where possible, any underlying cause of illness or ill-health before deciding on the appropriate oils and the necessary amount. As this takes training, it is not really practicable to do it yourself, but as long as the person you intend to massage is in reasonably good health, four drops of essential oil to fifteen millilitres (about two-and-a-half teaspoons) of carrier oil should be fine (use less of the powerful oils – see 'A Cautionary Note'). Please don't attempt to use massage on babies or children without first either taking professional advice or reading a good book on aromatherapy. It is possible to ingest essential oils, but this should *never* be done without professional advice.

### A Note about Synergy

Essential oils are more powerful in effect when blended together than they are on their own: such synergistic blends are usually carefully mixed by the professional aromatherapist to be used by specific individuals for specific purposes. However, it is both possible, and a lot of fun, to try this at home. Check the following list of essential oils to decide what effect you are aiming for. If, for example, you want something to relieve stress and help you relax try a blend of chamomile, lavender and geranium. If you find yourself surrounded by people with coughs and colds, use a few drops of eucalyptus, tea tree and cedarwood in a fragrancer to help keep germs at bay. Remember that essential oils are concentrated, so don't use too much, and experiment until you have a blend that smells good to you. It is also advisable to make a note of how many drops of each oil you use, in case you want to mix the blend another time. Ideally, try not to mix more than six different oils at a time.

## Essential Oils

Essential oils are extracted from well over 200 different plants, but many of these are not generally available or really only of interest to the perfume industry. There are about 50 in regular use in aromatherapy: here are some which can easily be used at home.

### Basil
(*Ocimum basilicum*)
Basil oil has a venerable history. It was mixed with other herbs by the ancient Egyptians for their mummification practices, the ancient Greeks used it in baths and massages, while in India it is reputed to protect the soul. The oil is extracted from the leaves by steam distillation.

Basil oil is antiviral and tonic, and beneficial in the treatment of colds, fevers and bronchitis: it also helps ease the pain of indigestion. It invigorates, and used in the bath can revitalise the skin and improve the circulation. However, it acts as a depressant if over-used, so employ sparingly and not too often.

Emotionally, basil energises the mind and body, and lifts depression.

### Bergamot
(*Citrus bergamia*)
Originally from Morocco, bergamot's therapeutic virtues were not recognised until it was introduced into Italy. Please note that *Citrus bergamia* is an entirely different plant from the herb red bergamot (*Monarda didyma*), which is the principal ingredient in Oswego Tea and the variety most often grown in the garden. The oil is expressed from the fruit.

Bergamot is antiseptic and cooling: it can be effective in treating sore throats and mouth infections, skin problems, and in lowering the temperature in feverish illnesses. However, it can irritate the skin, so should be used with care and sparingly, especially by those with sensitive skin.

Emotionally, bergamot is refreshing and enlivening. To me, bergamot oil smells like sticky lemon cake: it is a wonderful oil to use in a fragrancer when having friends round for coffee and biscuits.

## Cedarwood
*(Cedrus atlantica, Juniperus virginiana)*

Cedarwood oil is another of the ingredients used by the Egyptians in their embalming practices. Its strong antiseptic properties and wonderful rich, woody aroma made it popular and highly valued for cosmetics. The oil was originally taken from the cedar of Lebanon, but over-felling of the tree for use in furniture making resulted in it becoming extremely rare, and today the red cedar – grown principally in the USA and North Africa – is used instead. The oil is extracted from offcuts and woodchips by steam distillation.

Cedarwood essential oil is healing and regenerating, effective in the treatment of acne and eczema, and hair problems such as alopecia and dandruff. Be careful not to over-use the oil, however, as it can irritate the skin.

Cedarwood oil enhances and enlivens a low libido, making it a useful addition to any fragrance used in the bedroom – especially after a hard day at work!

## Chamomile

There are three different chamomile essential oils available, each with different properties: it's important to buy the right one for the right purpose.

Chamomile German (*Matricaria chamomilla*) is the 'strongest' of the three, and is not recommended for use with children. Chamomile Roman (*Anthemis nobilis*) is very gentle (and very expensive) and particularly safe for children, if used properly. Moroccan Chamomile (*Ormenis mixta*) is not recognised as being a true chamomile. To date there has been rather less research carried out on it than on the others, but it appears to have similar qualities to Chamomile Roman (although in lesser quantities) and may be used as a substitute – it is less expensive. It would be wiser not to use it to treat children, however, until more is known.

The details given here apply to Chamomile Roman. The flower was sacred to the sun in ancient Egypt, and used in the treatment of fits and fevers. The oil is extracted from the flowers by steam distillation.

Chamomile is powerfully anti-inflammatory, soothing, and mildly analgesic, making it highly beneficial in the treatment of dry and sensitive skin, nappy rash, muscular aches and cramps, arthritis and rheumatism. It can also alleviate diarrhoea, stomach ailments and colic. Its use as a comforting tisane has been known for centuries, and a massage with chamomile, or a cup of chamomile tea, before you go to bed or when you're feeling stressed, is an excellent sedative.

Emotionally, chamomile is relaxing and calming, easing depression, anxiety and irritation, and is particularly good for soothing fractious children.

## Cypress
(*Cupressus sempervirens*)
The aromatic wood of this evergreen tree was used by the ancient Egyptians to make their coffins, while the oil was used medicinally. The ancient Chinese chewed on the cones to help prevent loss of teeth and gingivitis. The oil is extracted from the needles, cones and twigs by steam distillation.

Cypress is antiseptic and soothing; it is beneficial for circulatory problems, varicose veins, eczema, and excessive sweating. It should not be used by anyone suffering from high blood pressure.

Emotionally, cypress is soothing and sedative, and is often used to help the bereaved overcome their grief and move on. Cypress oil is one of my favourites; it has a wonderful deep, rich, dark perfume – to me it smells pinier than pine oil itself!

## Eucalyptus
(*Eucalyptus globulus*)
Originally from Australia, eucalyptus is a fast-growing tree from whose leaves oil evaporates in the sun, resulting in an aromatic blue haze – from which the Blue Mountains of New South Wales take their name. It is likely that the Aborigines were the first to experiment with the therapeutic qualities of the oil. This is extracted from the leaves by steam distillation.

Eucalyptus is antiseptic, anti-inflammatory and decongestant, beneficial in the treatment of coughs, colds, sinusitis and throat infections. It also has antiviral and anti-bacterial qualities, and can help reduce fever.

Emotionally, eucalyptus is invigorating and uplifting, preventing drowsiness and stimulating the mind.

## Fennel
(*Foeniculum vulgare*)

The ancient Romans and Greeks used fennel seeds to sweeten the breath, kill fleas, and generally repel bad luck and promote personal strength of body. Today, fennel leaves are incorporated in classic fish dishes, while the seeds are used in the production of liquorice. The oil is extracted from the crushed seeds by steam distillation.

Fennel is extremely beneficial for all kinds of stomach problems: it is analgesic, antispasmodic, diuretic and a mild laxative. It is effective in the treatment of indigestion, colic, flatulence, nausea, obesity and kidney stones.

Emotionally, fennel oil is cheering and uplifting (unless, like me, you can't abide the smell of liquorice!)

## Frankincense
(*Boswellia thurifera*)

In ancient times frankincense (and myrrh – see below) were ranked with precious stones as highly valuable commodities, not just as incenses for solemn religious rituals, but also for their antiseptic and healing properties (originally the resins were burned in sick rooms to clear the air and repel illness). The method of obtaining the resin is ethically dubious – strips of the inner bark of the tree are cut away repeatedly: in defence, the tree 'bleeds' resin, which hardens on contact with air. The essential oil is then extracted from the tears of resin by steam distillation. Both frankincense and myrrh smell glorious, and have powerful healing abilities. If you choose to add them to your collection (and bear in mind that they are both very expensive), please use them sparingly and with appropriate respect.

Frankincense stimulates the immune system, and is particularly effective in the treatment of open wounds and ulcers by promoting the production (and afterwards reduction) of scar tissue. The oil is analgesic and anti-inflammatory, and can also be used in the treatment of coughs and bronchitis.

Emotionally, frankincense is extraordinarily uplifting and a powerful antidepressant, ideal to use in a fragrancer whenever you feel life has become just a little too much to cope with. That being said, if you suspect you may be suffering from clinical depression, please take professional advice.

## Geranium
(*Pelargonium graveolens*)
The geranium originated in Africa: it was not brought to Europe until the end of the 17th century. Although there are over 700 species, only two are commonly used in aromatherapy. Historically, the oil was used in the treatment of burns and open wounds. The oil is extracted from the leaves by steam distillation.

The essential oil is cleansing and antiseptic, easing skin inflammations and acne and helping normalise sebum production. It can help regulate hormone production, making it especially useful for women suffering from PMS and menopausal difficulties.

Geranium is both calming and uplifting, making it particularly useful in the treatment of stress and nervous tension. (Unfortunately, I simply cannot stand the smell of geranium, so its marvellous effects are completely lost to me!)

## Grapefruit
(*Citrus paradisi*)
Grapefruit (so called because the fruit grows in bunches of three or more and slightly resembles bunches of grapes when on the plant) is an evergreen tree, originally from Asia but now grown mainly in the USA. The fruit is a good source of vitamin C. The oil is extracted from the flesh by expression.

Grapefruit oil is mildly diuretic. It is also helpful in fighting cellulite and can either be added to the bathwater or massaged in a carrier oil into those difficult areas. It is also a good air disinfectant when diluted in water and sprayed around the house – and leaves a wonderful fresh, clean smell behind. Grapefruit essential oil has a short shelf-life, so do not be afraid to use it liberally!

Grapefruit is stimulating and invigorating, and makes a very pleasant addition to a winter fragrancer mix.

### Juniper
(*Juniperus communis*)
Juniper is a widespread shrub and one of the UK's native conifers, but it grows almost everywhere – North America, Asia, Europe and Africa. Juniper oil was one of the aromatics used in the mummification process by the ancient Egyptians. The leaves and berries were burned as incense in religious rituals, while in medieval Europe branches were burned to ward off evil. The berries are still used to flavour gin. The oil is extracted from the ripe berries by steam distillation. Juniper berry oil is the one to buy. Juniper oil is made from the leaves and twigs as well as the berries, and although cheaper, is of lesser quality – and smells nowhere near as wonderful.

Juniper is calming to the mind and a tonic to the body; it helps to lower blood pressure, relieve water retention and cellulite, and is beneficial for acne as well as greasy hair and skin. It is a great oil for those watching their weight. I use six drops of a juniper/grapefruit/basil blend in the bath – marvellous for the skin and to help improve those less than perfect areas of the body; and when used in a fragrancer, it leaves the whole body feeling refreshed. Juniper promotes trouble-free menstruation, so to be on the safe side, do not use the oil if you are pregnant (or trying to conceive). It can also overstimulate the kidneys, so avoid it if you have kidney problems.

Juniper alleviates anxiety, panic attacks, insomnia, and general mental tiredness.

### Lavender
(*Lavandula officinalis*)
Lavender has been used as a perfume throughout historical times (and probably in prehistoric times, too). The Romans used lavender water daily when bathing, and both Greeks and Romans burned lavender twigs to ward off disease. In England in the Middle Ages, newly washed clothes were laid on lavender bushes to dry, something that can still be done today. It imparts a wonderful, delicate scent of

lavender to articles of clothing, making them a joy to wear. The essential oil is extracted from the flowering tops by steam distillation.

Lavender is an exceptionally potent oil, yet at the same time so gentle that it can be safely used undiluted on the skin. It promotes skin growth and helps prevent scarring, and is extremely useful in the treatment of burns. Keep the burnt area under very cold water for ten minutes to cool, then place two drops of the oil on the burn and cover with clean gauze. Repeat as required. The oil is anti-inflammatory and antiseptic, and can be inhaled from a fragrancer or tissue to ease colds, sinus problems and flu. In massage it helps relieve aches and pains, rheumatism, water retention, headaches and migraine.

On an emotional level, lavender is soothing, helping to relieve stress and insomnia. It lifts the spirits and promotes inner harmony.

**Lemon**
*(Citrus limon)*
In the days of the tall ships, craft destined for long sea voyages were stocked with lemons to help prevent scurvy and to purify drinking water: lemon's astringent and antiseptic properties have been known, it would seem, since time immemorial. The essential oil is extracted from the skin by expression.

Lemon is anti-inflammatory, antiviral, astringent and diuretic, an invaluable addition to the household. Effective in the treatment of skin problems (especially those connected with the over-production of sebum), boils, warts and verrucas, lemon also eases colds, high blood pressure and fevers. Used in a fragrancer it acts as an insect repellent.

Lemon is stimulating and invigorating and particularly useful for helping drivers stay alert on long motorway journeys.

**Lemongrass**
*(Cymbopogon citratus)*
Lemongrass has been used as a seasoning in Thai and other Oriental recipes for centuries, and has recently become known in the West through the upsurge of interest in experimenting with new culinary experiences. The dried leaves can be burned to help keep the mind alert. The essential oil is extracted from the leaves by steam distillation.

Lemongrass is antibacterial, cooling and deodorising, and can act as an insect-repellent. In massage, it is beneficial for skin complaints associated with the overproduction of sebum, and also for relieving sore throats, while used in a vaporiser it helps ease respiratory problems. It can also alleviate athlete's foot, and may be used to deodorise footwear.

Emotionally, lemongrass is energising and stimulating, ideal for those who enjoy indoor exercises such as aerobics or general work-outs.

**Myrrh**

(*Commiphora myrrha*)

For details of the processing and extraction of myrrh, please see frankincense, above.

The ancient Egyptians and the Greeks both prized myrrh, employing it in religious and celebratory rituals, and in perfumes and medicines.

Myrrh essential oil is anti-fungal and anti-inflammatory, beneficial in the treatment of candida and athlete's foot, and to ease colds, catarrh and bronchial infections. It also has a moisturising effect, which in combination with its other qualities makes it effective for treating dry skin conditions.

Emotionally, myrrh has a calming, soothing effect, and can help ease insomnia and promote restful sleep.

**Neroli**

(*Citrus aurantium*)

Better known as orange blossom, neroli was probably first used by the Romans. The tree originated in China, but is now widespread in the USA, Algeria and around the Mediterranean. Being one of the low-yield oils, neroli is expensive to produce and buy (*Neroli bigarade* is the highest quality oil).

Neroli is bactericidal, sedative and antidepressant, effective in the treatment of shock, hysteria, panic attacks, depression, PMS and anxiety, and an excellent oil for combating broken veins, varicose veins, dry or ageing skin, and acne.

Neroli oil is relaxing, calming and emotionally uplifting, a wonderful fragrance for overcoming timidity and shyness.

## Patchouli
(*Pogostemon patchouli*)

Patchouli essential oil comes from the leaves of the small Indian shrub: the oil is concentrated in the three newest pairs of leaves. The rich, spicy, exotic fragrance was used to perfume blankets and shawls in India. Patchouli is used as a fixative in the perfume industry; the fragrance becomes more intense with age. The essential oil is extracted from the leaves by steam distillation.

Patchouli essential oil is anti-fungal, anti-inflammatory and bactericidal, effective in the treatment of skin problems such as eczema, acne, dandruff, and cracked, broken or abraded skin (it promotes the growth of new skin).

Patchouli is also an aphrodisiac, one of the reasons for its adoption by the 'Free Love' hippie generation of the 1960s! Emotionally, in small doses it is an uplifting, stimulating perfume: in larger doses it acts as a sedative.

## Peppermint
(*Mentha piperata*)

Used to flavour wine and food in ancient Egypt, peppermint has been renowned for centuries for its beneficial effects on the digestive system. The essential oil is extracted from the leaves by steam distillation.

Peppermint is antiseptic and antispasmodic, cooling and cleansing. It is effective in the treatment of respiratory problems of all types, and relieves indigestion, heartburn, flatulence, and the miseries associated with irritable bowel syndrome. It also helps ease skin disorders and can also be used as an insect repellent. If you suffer from epilepsy, either avoid peppermint oil or take advice from a professional.

Peppermint has a delightful fresh, clean fragrance, and is emotionally stimulating, strengthening and uplifting.

## Pine
(*Pinus sylvestris*)

Pine has been used in Scandinavian countries for almost as long as saunas have existed: the cones and needles are added to the heat source to invigorate, disinfect and refresh the atmosphere inside the room. Pine wood burned on an open fire has an almost magical effect. It is warm and resinous with a fresh top note redolent of walks on crisp winter days.

Pine oil is antiseptic, very effective in treating respiratory problems – colds, bronchitis, sinusitis – and, if used with a vaporiser, has been found to decrease the likelihood of infection in burns. It is also used extensively in household products, both as a disinfectant and a fragrance. Pine is usually regarded as a very 'masculine' aroma, used to perfume men's toiletries and cosmetics.

It has a stimulating, invigorating effect on the mind and emotions.

## Rose

(*Rosa centifolia*, *Rosa damascena*)

The overall effects of the essential oils of both these types of rose is the same: *Rosa centifolia* (a cabbage rose) produces a higher yield of oil than the *damascena*, which is the original source of the essential oil (and therefore, through a combination of traditional values and yield, the more expensive to buy). The most highly prized rose oil comes from Bulgaria. The rose has been known and deeply loved throughout history as the Queen of Flowers.[9]

The essential oil was most probably the first ever deliberately extracted from any plant. It is powerfully antiseptic and tonic, yet gentle enough to be used for children. Effective in the treatment of skin problems, especially those experienced by more mature skins, rose essential oil is also excellent for alleviating circulatory, menstrual and menopausal problems. It is generally agreed to be the perfect oil for women of all ages.

Emotionally, rose oil acts as an aphrodisiac and mood balancer. Try a couple of drops in a fragrancer or the bath when feeling weepy or angry for no apparent reason.

## Rosemary

(*Rosmarinus officinalis*)

A firm favourite of the ancient Egyptians, rosemary was also loved by the Romans and Greeks, for whom it symbolised love and death (which is probably the origin of its enduring meaning – 'remembrance'). It was one of the herbs worn around the neck to avert disease in time of plague.

Rosemary is astringent, antiseptic and cleansing. It improves the circulation, relieves constipation and stomach pains, eases general fatigue, stimulates the liver, and acts as a tonic for the hair (helping to prevent dandruff and hair loss when used in a final rinse). It also acts to raise the blood pressure, so if you suffer from hypertension, it would be wise to avoid it.

Rosemary stimulates the memory and clears the mind, fostering concentration and problem-solving abilities. It is a good oil to use in a fragrancer when studying for exams.

## Rosewood

### (*Aniba rosaeodora*)

The oil is extracted from the wood of the tree. I have read that in the environmentally sensitive areas of Brazil in which it grew, the tree is an endangered species (an attempt to reforest using new rosewood trees failed due to degraded soil conditions, themselves due to deforestation). I bought my rosewood oil before I knew this: I shall use it with respect and will not now replace it until I am sure I can do so without collaborating in such environmental damage. (Apparently, there is a substitute available, a blend of other oils that have practically the same effect and fragrance, but it's not easy to find at the time of writing.)

Rosewood oil is antiviral, astringent and bactericidal, good for all types of skin, but especially dry and mature.

Emotionally it is uplifting and relaxing, with a lovely rosy fragrance.

## Sandalwood

### (*Santalum album*)

Sandalwood oil has been used for thousands of years in China, Egypt and India in cosmetics, and in Indian temples. Traditionally, the furniture of King Solomon's great temple in Jerusalem was made from the wood. In India, the felling of the trees for distillation purposes is currently controlled by the government, and for each tree felled another is planted. The oil is extracted from the wood by steam distillation.

Sandalwood oil is soothing, anti-inflammatory and antiseptic, and effective in the treatment of sunburn, nettle rash, bronchitis and asthma. It helps to relieve itching (especially haemorrhoids and varicose veins), and to ease nausea and suppress vomiting.

The oil has a warm, woody smell, and emotionally is very helpful in raising low spirits and relieving anxiety. It also has the reputation of being an effective aphrodisiac.

### Tea Tree
*(Melaleuca alternifolia)*
Used for centuries by the Australian Aborigines in poultices for wounds and ulcers, and to treat infections and snakebite, tea tree essential oil is an extremely powerful antiseptic – at least twelve times as strong as carbolic acid (and much more pleasant to use!) The oil is extracted from the leaves by steam distillation.

Tea tree oil is antiviral, antifungal, bactericidal and hypo-allergenic: it is used to treat a wide range of ailments including athlete's foot, verrucas, colds, flu, gum disease, boils, rashes, sunburn and mouth ulcers (when diluted in water as a mouthwash). It is also very effective in the kitchen – use a couple of drops in warm water to clean and disinfect working surfaces and floors, and can be used in a plant mister to spray a fine disinfectant mist onto carpets. Tea tree is a good insect repellent and can help keep fleas under control in pet-owning households.

Tea tree is valued for its physical rather than emotional properties, but it has a pleasant aroma (similar to eucalyptus but milder) and when used in a fragrancer is cleansing and reassuring.

### Ylang-Ylang
*(Cananga odorata)*
The tree is native to Indonesia and the Philippines, and can grow to a height of 60 feet (20 metres). The flowers should be picked early in the morning, and were traditionally mixed with coconut oil for use as a fragrant conditioner for the skin and hair. Medicinally, the oil was used to combat malaria, skin infections and insect stings. The oil is extracted from the flowers by steam distillation.

Essential oil of ylang-ylang is antiseptic, and can be beneficial in the treatment of high blood pressure and troublesome skin conditions.

Ylang-ylang smells wonderful, similar to jasmine, but heavier. Its warm, sensual fragrance is excellent for easing anxiety and depression, and – used as a perfume – can assist sufferers of frigidity and impotence. (The oil is an aphrodisiac and is used extensively in the perfume industry.) In small amounts it is effective as a stress-reliever and to alleviate insomnia.

## Aromatherapy in the Home

By far the easiest way to reap the benefits of aromatherapy in your own home is to use a vaporiser. These use heat to vaporise the oils, usually mixed with water, which then disperse throughout the room (or the whole house, if you leave the internal doors open). There are several different types of vaporiser.

**Fragrancers** which use a night light are perhaps the most readily available. Try to find one with a deep dish or small bowl to hold the oil and water mix: it needs less attention than the shallower type since it takes longer for the liquid to evaporate. Make sure the fragrancer is placed somewhere safe, out of the reach of children or animals, somewhere it cannot be knocked over, and away from paper or other flammable materials. Electric vaporisers are available, but are more expensive and, of course, require a power source.

**Humidifiers** are another option. The old-fashioned sort that hold water and hook over a warm radiator are excellent, and avoid the expense of running an electric humidifier (although, of course, this is only effective in the colder months, when the radiator is actually working! Also, some modern radiator designs might not be suitable for this method.) Add a couple of drops of your favourite oil or oil mix to spread a gentle perfume throughout your home. If you cannot find a humidifier but like the idea of using the radiator, several drops of your favourite oil mix on a ball of cotton wool, tucked behind the radiator, works just as well, although the fragrance will be more intense and not last quite so long.

**Perfume rings**, small, hollow pottery rings that are designed to sit on a light bulb and use its heat to diffuse the oil's aroma, can be fiddly to use and even dangerous if sufficient care is not taken when using them. Essential oils are flammable, and the heat from the light bulb can set them alight if they touch the hot glass.

When employing any method that requires heating the oils, make sure the vaporiser has a non-porous inner surface so that it can be thoroughly cleaned between uses.

**Scented candles** have proved enduringly popular, although most of those commercially available are made with synthetic perfumes rather than essential oils. It is possible to add your chosen oil or oil mix to an ordinary candle – wait until the wax has warmed and softened, then carefully add the oil, making sure none touches the lit wick – but it is not an easy operation. A steady hand and concentration are required if you are not to set fire to your hair! However, it is possible to make your own aromatherapy candles – see Chapter Nine, Crafty Perfumes! for more details. Generally speaking and for safety's sake, other methods of diffusing the fragrance by using heat are preferable.

**Spraying** the rooms of the house is an inexpensive and easy way to use essential oils in the home. Using a new plant mister, add your chosen oils to water (five drops to every 300 millilitres of water), shake well, and lightly spray the room. Avoid spraying on wood, fish tanks, books or electrical equipment, particularly.[10]

### Aromatherapy and Basic Health

Obviously, any ailment or illness which gives you cause for concern should be investigated by your doctor or health professional, but there are a few simple aromatherapy treatments you can use at home which may alleviate the unpleasant symptoms of some common ailments.

The blocked sinuses of colds, flu and sinusitis can be relieved by inhaling pine, eucalyptus and/or lavender essential oils from a basin of very hot water. Add two or three drops of oil to the water, cover your head with a towel, lean over the basin – not too close to the water, and certainly not less than six inches above the surface when the water is at its hottest – and breathe deeply for a few minutes. Keep your eyes closed to avoid irritation.

A drop of lavender oil placed directly on a blister will prevent infection and speed up healing. A blister caused by a burn or scald can be eased by placing a couple of drops of lavender oil on the skin and then holding an ice cube over the blister for as long as possible. Remember that the blister forms to protect the raw, damaged skin underneath: never pierce or burst it.

For cuts, scratches and abrasions, bathing with warm water to which has been added a couple of drops of lavender and one of tea tree oil will gently cleanse and disinfect. Cover with a clean dressing, to which a drop or two of lavender has been added to speed up healing.

Massaging the temples with lavender, peppermint and/or rose in a small amount of carrier oil can help ease the pain of a headache. Breathing in the aroma of lavender or rose from a tissue can also help relieve the stress that may have caused or contributed to the headache in the first place.

Lavender, rose and chamomile are beneficial in cases of insomnia. A few drops of the neat oil on a tissue on a bedside cabinet or on a cotton wool ball tucked behind a radiator releases a soothing, calming fragrance into the room, promoting restful sleep.

## Aromatherapy and Beauty

As can be seen from the list earlier in this chapter, there are oils available for a host of different beauty problems, literally from head to toe!

Most people are familiar with herbal shampoos – rosemary for dark hair and chamomile for fair. Try adding a couple of drops of the appropriate essential oils to the final rinse when washing your hair. For normal hair, use lemon to keep the hair healthy and shining. Dry hair can benefit from rosemary or sandalwood. For greasy hair, cypress, basil or lemon are beneficial. Hair that has been damaged by perming or colouring needs the very gentlest handling – lavender and sandalwood are well worth a try. Dandruff can respond well to rosemary, cedarwood or patchouli oil. Add a drop of rosemary to a rinse for dark hair, and chamomile for fair hair. For red hair, try a little carrot or rose.

All types of skins benefit from being treated with natural ingredients rather than the chemicals most of us use, and this is perfectly safe as long as you follow some simple, commonsense guidelines. Most notably make sure you use oils appropriate for your skin type and the effect for which you are aiming; for example, if combating broken veins or wrinkles, use a carrier, and don't use too much!

A wonderful way of cleansing the skin is to use a combination of fruit and essential oils. For greasy skin with open pores and blackheads, a drop of lavender or rosewood oil in a tablespoonful of mashed pawpaw[11] is absolutely wonderful as a cleanser, leaving the skin spotlessly clean, clear and glowing with health. (The enzymes in the fruit effectively 'digest' dead skin cells and other debris.) Rub it gently onto the face and neck, avoiding the eye area, and leave for five minutes before rinsing off with tepid water. Do not use it on dry or sensitive skin, however – it is very strong. I have found that it will keep for a couple of weeks in the refrigerator in a small, scrupulously clean screwtop jar: it also freezes quite well, so I generally make up a mix using the whole pawpaw and four to six drops of oil, then freeze in ice-cube trays. Two cubes – thawed – are usually sufficient for one application. Mashed strawberry with a drop of rose, rosewood or sandalwood is a somewhat gentler astringent cleansing mask for the face. For well-balanced skins, use yoghurt, or a mix of yoghurt and oatmeal, as a base: for dry skins, substitute honey for the oatmeal.

Although it is possible to make your own cream cleansers, it is easier and less time-consuming to buy a suitable base (unperfumed, hypo-allergenic and preferably wholly natural: try a good health-food outlet or specialist shop) and add your own essential oils at home. Geranium and lavender are suitable for all types of skin: chamomile, rose, rosewood and sandalwood are beneficial for dry skin; juniper, cypress, lemon and rosemary for oily; neroli, fennel, myrrh and rose for ageing or wrinkled skin. For combination skins, use the appropriate oils for each zone.

Toners and fresheners can be made up by adding a drop or two of the essential oils (as detailed above) to an appropriate flower water (either bought or home-made[12]), and gently applied to the face with cotton wool or tissue. To moisturise, use your chosen oils in a vegetable oil carrier.

A very pleasant change from commercial bubblebaths and oils is to fill a small muslin bag with oatmeal, tie it under the hot tap and let the bathwater run. The result is a slightly milky bath which is wonderfully soothing and gently moisturising for the skin. If you also add your choice of essential oils to the water, you can pamper yourself with a treat for the mind, the senses and the body. If you prefer showers, add a drop or two of your oil to the oatmeal before closing the muslin, soak the bag for a moment in hot water, then rub the bag all over yourself while under the spray. The effect is less intense than in the bath, but still leaves you with beautifully smooth skin.

Our feet tend to take a lot of neglect. Hidden for most of the time in tights, socks and shoes, often hot, sweaty, constricted and uncomfortable, and subject to pressures, shocks and weight that would leave any other part of the body incapacitated – they deserve better. Essential oils that are particularly beneficial for the feet are peppermint and cypress (refreshing, and helps keep feet smelling sweet), tagetes (softens hard skin), lavender and fennel (revives tired feet and reduces swelling), and geranium (improves the circulation and fortifies the skin on the feet). Try adding a mix of oils to warm water and soaking the feet for ten minutes, and follow up with a massage with peppermint oil in sweet almond oil. It is worth while investing in a foot-massager. If you buy a wooden one, it is possible to place a few drops of cypress oil between the revolving beads, thus releasing the aroma as you gently roll your feet back and forth – a fragrantly relaxing exercise.

Of course, there are many other ways of employing aromatherapy to enhance your life,[13] but those noted here may inspire you to experiment and discover them for yourself – always the most satisfying way to learn.

# 4
# *Herbalism*

For tens of thousands of years, magic and herbalism were the only forms of medical treatment available to the human race. This is not really the place to explore the practice and processes of magic, except to note that much of it depended on the faith of the recipient: as with so many things, if the sufferer believed a spell or ritual would be effective in relieving or curing his ailment, in a large number of cases such proved to be the case.

Herbalism, however, is quite a different matter. Originally, the healing and nutritional properties of herbs were not differentiated: knowledge of the plants which alleviated illness and promoted health were handed down from generation to generation. As the centuries passed, through observation and experimentation, and no doubt with a lot of trial and error thrown in, our ancient ancestors learned the effects of different herbs on various human conditions. The first person who discovered that chewing willow bark (the original source of acetyl-salicylic acid – in other words, aspirin) relieved a multitude of aches and pains must have looked on it as a gift of the gods! (It's interesting to speculate whether the experiment might have been prompted by the sweet and comforting aroma given off by burning willow wood …)

Initially, native, easily obtained herbs and flowers were used by local populations. As movement between peoples – migration, military incursions and intermarriage between tribes – became a feature of life, a greater variety of herbs became available for all as the incoming folk brought seeds and young plants with them. The Romans were responsible for spreading some of the native Mediterranean herbs (lavender, rosemary, basil etc.) to other parts of Europe; and as trade between different continents grew, even more exotic species became known to herbalists and, later, their successors – the doctors.

Hippocrates, the 'Father of Medicine', was well-known as a teacher and physician in the 4th century BCE: he gave his name to the Hippocratic Oath, which sets out the duties and responsibilities of the doctor to his patients. In the 1st century BCE, Dioscorides wrote *De Materia Medica*, the first textbook to take the medicinal, toxic and curative properties of plants as its subject. The book remained the primary reference book for the next 1,600 years. The medical works of Galen of Pergamum, who lived in the latter half of the 2nd century CE, were influential in the medical world for 1,400 years – until the 16th century, when doubt began to be cast on his assumption that the human body was kept in balance by the four 'humours': blood, black bile, yellow bile and phlegm. The first true medical schools appeared in Italy and France in the 11th and 12th centuries, although untrained 'lay healers', herbalists in the main, still cared for the majority of the sick. It was not until the 19th century that medicine in the West became science-based.

## Chinese Herbal Medicine

Where Western medicine looked for physical causes for ill-health, in the East illness was considered to be the effect of a loss of the natural balance of *ch'i*. *Ch'i* is the universal life force that pervades all things, and has two forms: passive, cold, damp, dark, feminine *yin*, and active, hot, dry, light, masculine *yang*. As well as needing to have *ch'i* in balance within the body, it is necessary to have the elements in harmony as well. (In Chinese thought there are five elements as opposed to the four – fire, earth, air and water – with which the West is familiar.) The five elements each have a particular type of herb associated with them.

**Wood** herbs are sour and refreshing and relate to *yin*. They include hawthorn berries and rosehips, and affect the liver and the digestive system.

**Fire** herbs are bitter, and are considered *yin* and cooling to the body. They include dandelion leaves, the Chinese rhubarb and peony, and act to detoxify and fight infections. They also stimulate the digestive system.

**Earth** herbs are *yang*, sweet and warming, and include ginseng and angelica. They warm and soothe the body and act as a tonic.

**Metal** herbs are *yang*, spicy and drying, improving the circulation, alleviating arthritic pains, and stimulating digestion and overall energy and stamina. They include ginger, cinnamon and cloves.

**Water** herbs are salty and, naturally, believed to be *yin*. They are moistening and cooling to maintain the fluid balance in the body and assist the function of the kidneys. Water herbs include seaweeds and barley.

A practitioner of Chinese herbal medicine will carefully diagnose the patient's condition and prescribe a herbal mixture, which is most often drunk as a tea after being boiled in water for a specified amount of time. Chinese medicine uses over six thousand different plants, and must always be prescribed by an authorised practitioner. For example:

Burdock (*Arctium lappa*) helps the patient recover from infection: it is useful for arthritis and skin conditions, and is a muscle-relaxant.

Corydalis (*Corydalis solida*) has a sedative action, reducing stress, invigorating the circulation, and relieving menstrual pain.

Fringed Pink (*Dianthus superbus*) alleviates constipation and eczema, eases kidney and urinary tract complaints, and is a general tonic for the nervous system.

Honeysuckle (*Lonicera japonica*) reduces fever and treats inflammations, sores and dysentery.

The famous Chinese Peony (*Paeonia lactiflora*) has an abundance of uses in herbal medicine. The flower is antiviral and antibacterial, relieving cold sores and fevers: it is antispasmodic and calming, used to treat headaches, hysteria, epilepsy, panic attacks and the after-effects of nightmares. It is also used for menstrual disorders, to lower blood pressure, ease kidney and gall stones as well as liver ailments, and to heal wounds, sores, varicose veins and improve poor circulation. It should not be used during pregnancy. Like pennyroyal, it regulates menstrual problems.

## Other Floral Remedies

### Bach Flower Remedies

Edward Bach was a physician, trained in orthodox medicine, who practised homeopathy during the first half of the 20th century. His belief that the body, mind and spirit need to be operating in harmony for there to be health led him to explore the possibility of enabling individuals to use their inner resources to cure themselves, by providing them with remedies for stress, imbalance and a negative mindset. He found his remedies in the flowers of wild plants,[1] shrubs and trees.

The remedies are prepared by floating freshly picked flowers on pure spring water in full sunlight. After the requisite amount of time, the water is strained, alcohol added as a preservative and it is bottled and sold. Bach Flower Remedies should be diluted in spring water before being used.

Dr Bach's original belief – that a positive mental attitude has a highly beneficial effect on the physical body, allowing healing of physical ailments to take place – led him to group what he saw as the most common negative states of mind into seven categories: oversensitivity, loneliness, uncertainty, fear, despair (despondency), excessive concern for the welfare of others, and lack of interest in the present. These were further divided into a total of 38 'types' for which there is a corresponding remedy. Some of these, interestingly, reflect traditional correspondences. Oak,[2] for example, is the remedy for despondency for those whose strength would normally see them steadily through any illness or adversity, while Himalayan Balsam (which bears exploding seedpods in the autumn) is recommended to alleviate feelings of loneliness in people who are irritable, prone to temperamental outbursts, and want everything done immediately.

Bach Flower Remedies are regarded as being perfectly safe for everyone – even babies and animals – as long as they are diluted as recommended. It is less the active constituent of the plant material than the elusive 'life force' within the flowers that imbues the spring water with subtle healing energies. When deciding which remedies are correct for any particular individual, it is important to be entirely honest about the emotional state, circumstances and fundamental personality of the person involved – not that choosing the wrong remedy will cause any harm, but because it may delay recovery. That being said, it is a fairly well-known fact that if you *believe* something will cure you, 90% of the time it will do just that!

### Flower Essence Therapy

In some ways similar to the Bach Flower Remedies, Flower Essences – produced in and imported from California, USA – are created by immersing flower petals in sun-warmed water. The essences are claimed to possess harmonising and healing vibrations, gathered from the sun by the flowers, and to bring body, mind and spirit into equilibrium. Flower Essences range from *aloe vera* – claimed to increase an individual's sensitivity towards others – to zinnia, which is said to promote laughter as a powerful force for self-healing.[3]

# 5
# *Gardens*

*The kiss of the sun for pardon,*
*The song of the birds for mirth,*
*One is nearer God's Heart in a garden,*
*Than anywhere else on earth.*[1]

Whether the god concerned is Jesus Christ, or Cernunnos, Lord of the Greenwood, or the divinity that lives within us all, there is no denying that the garden occupies a very special place in the human psyche.

A garden is a place set apart from the stresses and toils of daily life. It is where we go to unwind and relax: eat lunch, read, feed the birds, watch the children play, or simply sit and soak up peace and tranquillity. It is somewhere you can go at any time and see something different: the cycle of the seasons brings its own delights, month after month, from the bright new green of spring to the holly and ivy of chilly winter – and all the perfumes and colours of the seasons in between.

Gardens, in one form or another, have been in existence for thousands of years. In neolithic times (from around 4000 BCE), when humans stopped being nomadic and settled down into stable communities, they grew the foodstuff they needed close to their campsites, in what were, essentially, the first 'kitchen gardens'. Wealthy Egyptians of the New Kingdom (which spanned the centuries from 1540 to 1075 BCE) owned gardens, laid out with a variety of trees and shrubs and often with a pool stocked with fish and ducks. Flowers were grown for their beauty alone in ancient Egypt, Sumer, Assyria and Babylonia. There were gardens in the ancient Roman and Greek civilisations, in China and Japan: they appeared anywhere, in fact, where humans stopped being nomadic and settled down into co-operative communities. Initially – indeed, for a considerable length of time – gardens were the preserve of the wealthy who could afford to keep gardeners to care for them. It was not until very recently (in the last two centuries) that other classes of society were able to own their own small plots. These days almost everyone has access to a garden, if not their own, then one of the innumerable parks and gardens that have been created in urban population centres.

And we all need them. No matter how highly sophisticated we become, there will always be a part of us that is entirely and honestly *animal*, needing fresh air, wind and clouds; contact with natural growing things; moving water and birdsong; plants and the feel of the native earth beneath our feet. To deny it is to run the very real risk of ulcers, heart complaints, skin problems – the vast array of physical ailments that result from stress and the artificial environments in which most of us work and far too many of us live.[2]

Gardens can be many things. Depending on who you are and what resources you have available, you may delight in the smell, taste, economy and sheer satisfaction of growing some of your own food in a kitchen garden. You may prefer the stately nobility of a formal garden, or the sweet-scented, rambling riotous growth of your own wildflower patch or mini-meadow. A well designed and infinitely useful herb garden may be more appealing, or an arbour created specifically to smell glorious throughout the summer months. You may even like to experiment with adaptations of garden designs from other parts of the world: a *feng shui* garden, perhaps, or a Mediterranean rockery. (I would suggest, however, not a Zen Rock Garden, which would rather defeat the object of this book!) And if you do not have access to a garden at all, do not despair. No matter where you live, if you have a window with access to some light, there will be a plant that you can grow indoors, bringing a little of its natural magic with it …

It is important to make a note of the conditions of your garden (which direction it faces, how much light or wind it gets, what sort of soil is present – and how much time and energy you will be able to devote to it!) before you decide what sort of garden you want. Although it is usually possible to change some of the factors – by digging in good organic compost to make a dry, sandy soil more water retentive and fertile, for example – to do so may require more of you than you can realistically give. Some plants have very specific soil, light and temperature requirements and will not flourish if these are not provided. Be practical, adaptable, and willing to experiment, and do not forget that you are dealing with living things. Treat them with respect and they will repay your care with years of fragrant beauty!

Plants, and therefore the gardens in which they grow, change and evolve with the passing seasons and years – try to bear this in mind when planning your own plot. If you wish to be able to enjoy your garden all year round, choose plants that provide interest in each season: conifers for winter green, deciduous shrubs for autumn and spring colour, bright flowers for the summer (there are suggestions in the section Fragrant Gardens, below). If you only intend to use the garden in the summer months, however, it is less important to plan for the entire year, although a little coniferous evergreen is a pleasing sight when everything else looks grey and dead. Some shrubs can grow and spread very quickly, as can some low-growing ground cover plants, so try to find out about the plants' growth before planting and plan the garden accordingly.

Remember, also, that many of your fragrant plants can be utilised even after you have enjoyed their beauty in the garden. See 'Crafty Perfumes!' for advice on preserving plant material and suggestions for its use in pot pourri, herb pillows and other home projects.

**Fragrant Gardens**

Practically all gardens are fragrant to some extent, but here we will focus on those designed specifically for their perfumed effect. It would be useful to incorporate some sort of seat into the overall design as simply sitting and breathing deeply of the perfume is a wonderfully tension-relieving therapy in itself. Ideally, if you have the space, try to include a water feature as well – and if you can incorporate a fountain or waterfall, too – so much the better. These produce negative ions, which are healthy and stimulating.

Before deciding exactly what sort of fragrant garden you would like, it is wise to visit a garden centre (or two) over the space of a few months – or even a year if you have the patience and determination – to see how different plants behave over time.

GARDENS

Although a haphazard garden can be absolutely charming, if you want something a little more formal, careful advance planning can save money, effort and time, not to mention disappointment. Bear in mind the space available, the climatic conditions for your part of the world, the amount of time you can devote to the garden, and the needs of the plant itself – and do not be afraid to ask for advice.

**The Romantic Garden**
The rose is – and traditionally always has been – the ultimate symbol of love in the floral world. Even its thorns have come to represent the trials and tribulations suffered by those in love. Its wonderful fragrance and extravagant beauty have appealed to lovers down through the ages, and in most countries of the world. The Japanese *Rosa rugosa* has been cultivated for over a thousand years; the wild roses of the British Isles have graced country hedgerows since time immemorial as well as inspiring a number of heraldic devices; the Damask roses of India and ancient Persia were most likely the first sources of attar of roses (rose essential oil); the Cherokee and Grant roses of the USA have their own romantic legends, while *Rosa chinensis*, the Chinese rose from which so many of our modern types have been developed, also has a long and venerable history.

There are a bewildering number of different forms of rose available (climbing, bush, miniature; Wild, Musk, Cabbage, Damask, Floribunda, Moss, Hybrid Tea …), in an astonishing variety of colours – but not all roses are scented. When choosing for your garden, check the fragrance first, then decide on the colour. You might even like to give a new slant to an old notion and select your roses according to the Language of Flowers:[3]

Thornless rose – Love without pain
White rose – Worthy of love
Pink rose – Grace and elegance
Red rose – Happy love
Deep red rose – Bashful or secret love
Purple-red rose – Unselfconscious beauty
Cream rose – Beauty forever new

'Blue' rose – Meeting by moonlight
Orange rose – Infatuation
Coral-coloured rose – Sexual desire
Yellow rose – Jealousy
Golden rose – Love's riches
Red and white roses together – United in love
Striped roses – Reconciliation
'Flushed' roses (vari-coloured) – Love growing steadily
Wild rose – Innocent love
Musk rose – Beautiful and capricious
Cabbage rose – Love is welcome
Damask rose – Seduction
Tea rose – Dignity
Floribunda – Energy and cheerfulness
Moss rose – Luxury

When choosing the roses, bear in mind that some have a very short flowering period while others can last for months. These details may be included in the planting and care instructions that come with the plant: if not, ask for advice or refer to a specialist publication. Sometimes it may be more personally satisfying to have one or two intensely perfumed but short-lived roses than an entire garden of bushes with less meaningful fragrances: it is always a matter of personal preference. Remember, too, that once the rose petals are past their best and loose on the flower, they can be picked, dried, and used to make floral sachets, herb pillows, and *pot pourri*.[4]

The bases of rose plants often become bare of leaves and branches as they mature. Underplanting with other vegetation (my preference is either for dark green, glossy ferns or a herb like Lemon Balm (*Melissa*) depending on how much light is available) will make the area look a little less unloved and cut down on the amount of bare earth available for weeds to grow.

Take the time to enjoy your rose garden. It is an expression of love – for yourself, for your loved ones, for the flowers themselves, such beautiful ambassadors of the natural world. As you soak up the serenity of the place, fill your lungs with its perfume and your mind and heart with love.

### Fragrant Flowers

Not all flowers are perfumed – many rely on their colour to attract the insects that pollinate them – but the following selection lists some of the most common fragranced flowers that can be easily grown in the garden. Most of the flowers noted here can be used in *pot pourri*, and some can be used to make wine.[5]

**Carnations and Pinks** (*Dianthus*) are available in a great variety of colours and types, from tight, monochromatic flower-heads, through stripes and flecks, to multi-coloured softly flushed lacy flowers. Their sweet perfume varies from light and delicate to heavily fragrant. In the language of flowers, when presented in a posy or as a corsage or buttonhole, a red carnation symbolises love at first sight, a yellow one means 'disdain', while a striped carnation represents affection spurned. It is probably safe to disregard this in the garden, however!

**Freesias** are extraordinarily fragrant, with an intense, slightly exotic perfume and warm, richly coloured, creamy flowers. They are quite delicate, however, and not worth trying to grow outdoors unless the garden is in a warm, sheltered, southern area.

**Gardenia** (*Gardenia*) is perhaps not suitable for all gardens – it can grow quite tall, requires a warm, sheltered spot and care and attention – but as a specimen plant in an otherwise fairly simple garden (or grown in a conservatory, sunroom or greenhouse) it can be quite stunning. The rich, sweet perfume and big, creamy flowers add a gloriously exotic note to any garden.

**Honeysuckle** (*Lonicera*), that fragrant native of country hedgerows, has been hybridised to create longer-lasting, more intensely scented garden climbing shrubs which are available from most garden centres. The sight and smell of honeysuckle rambling over and through a fence or hedge, its trumpet-shaped flowers flickering like tiny tongues of golden flame amongst the bright green of its foliage, epitomises warm summer days. In the language of flowers, honeysuckle symbolises tenderness and the ties of affection, making it a perfect secondary plant for a romantic garden.

**Jasmine** (*Jasminum officinalis*), despite its delicate appearance and sub-tropical origin, is actually quite a tough plant, and will grow in sheltered spots in temperate zones. Planted against a wall where it can scramble up a trellis, it will scent the air deliciously in summer.

Stephanotis flowers resemble jasmine in shape, but are larger and waxy: the leaves are large and dark, glossy green. The plant grows and spreads fairly quickly, and has a sweet, jasmine-like scent. For a truly stunning effect in the garden, try growing it over an arbour with a bench, where you can sit and enjoy the fragrance.

**Lavender** (*Lavandula*) – there are several different types of this venerable and much-loved plant, all (with one exception – *Lavandula multifida* – which smells of oregano) with the distinctive fragrance of lavender, but with slightly different habits and appearances: some grow as small bushes, others are ideal to create perfumed hedges. It is best to find out which is most appropriate for your purposes before buying.

**Lupin** (*Arboreus*) is tall, fragrant, very colourful, and requires little care and attention. However, the plant – and particularly the seeds – are poisonous, so take care if the garden is to be enjoyed by children as well as adults.

**Magnolia**, that beautiful, opulent native of Asia and North America, is available in a variety of different types, from the magnificent tree with its blushing, creamy, richly scented flowers which seem to demand the viewer's whole attention (and thus really should be grown as a specimen plant or with the minimum of other plants), to the much smaller *stellata*, whose pure white, wonderfully fragrant flowers have beautifully frilled and serrated edges. Magnolias can grow to a considerable age, so it is best to be certain you can cope with such a long-term plant companion before acquiring one.

**Nemesia** (*foetens* variety), a low-growing bedding plant with flowers in a host of bright colours, is a fragrant option for beside paths or to underplant taller plants.

**Nicotiana**, which is at its most fragrant in the evening, is available in a limited range of colours, but the gloriously rich, intense fragrance fills the air on warm summer evenings. The plant is ideal as a secondary perfume for the Romantic Garden – for balmy nights under the stars with a loved one.

**Passion Flower** (*Passiflora*), which comes in a variety of delightful forms and colours, is a fragrant climber with complex and beautiful flowers followed by the famous fruit. Native to tropical regions of America (Mexico to Brazil), it can be grown in warm, sheltered areas of temperate zones. In particularly long, hot summers it will even fruit out of doors in Britain – though that may be due to global climatic change rather than the plant's adaptability. There are two explanations given for the plant's name. Firstly, the fruit is reputed to inspire passion in anyone who eats it, and secondly, the flowers of the most common varieties have been compared, somewhat fancifully, to symbols of Christ's Passion on the Cross, various parts of the flower being identified with the crown of thorns, the five wounds etc.

**Peony** (*Paeonia*) – one of the oldest plants used in gardens – has a variety of different types and colours, all with large, luxurious and often fragrant flowers. (Check that the variety is perfumed before acquiring it.) Peonies add an element of opulence to a garden without overpowering it. The bush has a maximum height of about a metre, requires little attention in a reasonably well-kept garden, and can live for fifty years or more.

**Stocks** (*Matthiola*), with their concentrated spicy-sweet, slightly clove-like perfume, are a sheer delight. They do have a somewhat old-fashioned, 'fussy' appearance, however, and may look a little out of place in a simple or modern-styled garden. For twenty-four-hour fragrance, plant Night Scented Stock (*Matthiola bicornis*) as well. As its name suggests, smells sweetest at night: the fragrance is faintly reminiscent of jasmine. Night scented stocks are annuals, easily grown from seed, and really deserve a place in any garden – not so much for their flowers, which are a dull, pale, pinkish colour – but for the glorious aroma that drifts in through the open windows on summer evenings.

**Sweet Pea** (*Lathyrus odoratus*) is available in almost every colour imaginable (except green). It is a climber and usually needs tying to supports (perhaps a fence or trellis, or try growing it through shrubs or small trees, tying it very loosely to the branches), but the wonderful fragrance is well worth the extra care and attention. The flowers are beautiful, from a distance resembling a dance of butterflies.

**Wallflower** (*Cheiranthus*) is a small but richly coloured plant with a lovely fragrance. It is ideal for growing in borders, or just under a window so that the perfume can drift in on warm, sunny days.

**Wisteria** (*W. sinensis*) is a beautiful, graceful shrub which needs considerable support and some attention as it grows, and is therefore not really suitable for small gardens or those with little time to devote to its care. As a backdrop to a garden with an Oriental feel, however, it can hardly be bettered, and its fragrant, pendulous, pale indigo flowers are a sheer delight.

**Violas and Violets**, small, sweetly perfumed plants that are ideal for edging paths and borders, have now been bred to appear in many more colours than the traditional purple or white. Not all are fragranced, so it is best to smell before you buy. The mauve shades represent faithfulness and modesty, the white purity of intent, and the yellow, 'rural happiness'.

## Year Long Floral Fragrance

It is quite possible to have a fragrant garden all year round – you simply need to grow plants that flower at different times of the year.

### Spring
Plant early spring bulbs in the autumn before the spring in which you want them to flower. Scented narcissi, hyacinths and lily of the valley are some of the most easily obtainable and fragrant. Magnolia, that ancient and sweetly scented shrub, blooms early in the year. Its large creamy flowers look striking against the new green of spring, and there are so many varieties that it should be possible to find one that will fit into a small garden. If you are lucky enough to own a large garden, a linden tree can make a wonderfully fragrant feature. Peonies begin to flower at the end of the spring, acting as a fragrant reminder that summer is near.

### Summer
Late spring through to early autumn is the time when most flowers blossom. Lilac, rose, honeysuckle, the choice is almost endless. See the list of Fragrant Flowers – above – or try to visit a garden centre or nursery and spend some time enjoying 'smelling the flowers'.

### Autumn
Autumn is a time for colour more than scent (understandably, the flowers that employ insects to pollinate them have mostly died along

with the insects themselves) especially after a long, hot summer when the deciduous plants – trees, shrubs, creepers etc. – have been a blaze of vibrant colour. However, lavender is still in flower to act as a standby until the winter flowers appear. My eucalyptus also flowers at this time of year: the flowers have a strange, musky fragrance that I find quite evocative, although I can imagine others finding it unpleasant.

### Winter

There are only a few scented plants that flower in the winter, but they certainly brighten up long, cold days. The best known are varieties of *Daphne* (named after the chaste nymph who, when pursued by Apollo, begged Gaea to rescue her: the earth goddess changed her into a fragrant tree) and the well-known *Mahonia*, whose sprays of little yellow flowers have a perfume faintly reminiscent of lily of the valley. Sweet violet (*Viola odorata*) flowers from late winter to the middle of spring, bringing a welcome hint of colour and fragrance to the winter garden.

### The Herbal Garden

Herbs are, basically, green plants, which strictly speaking die back at the end of their growing season. However, over time the word has come to mean plants that have a particular use for humans, whether to flavour food or medicinally. These herbs usually have aromatic foliage which releases its fragrance – as an essential oil – when bruised. Most people are familiar with a number of common culinary herbs, even if only from the packaging of ready-prepared meals such as fish in parsley sauce, or from the words of traditional songs like 'Scarborough Fair'.[6] But there are many others, both culinary and a little more unusual, which can be used to add a very special element to the garden and, of course, many herbs can be grown on the kitchen windowsill.

### The Kitchen Herb Garden

**Basil** (*Ocimum basilicum*) has been used as a culinary herb since time immemorial. Known as the King of Herbs, it has a unique and truly wonderful fragrance and taste. (Try a summer sandwich of sliced tomato and just-picked basil leaves ...) It is an annual herb (needs to be grown afresh every year) and, unusually, is impossible to dry – or rather, it can be dried, but the flavour changes so substantially in the process that it ends up tasting nothing like the original. I have tried freezing it, but it loses a lot of its savour. Basil is, therefore, an ephemeral and short-lived treasure, to be relished throughout the summer, and looked forward to during the cold months.

Basil requires considerable care to be grown out of doors – a lot of sun, hot weather, enough water, and shelter from the wind. In the UK, it is better grown in a large pot on the kitchen windowsill and the leaves picked as required. Nip out the tops to keep it bushy. I rank it as indispensable in the kitchen. Add the leaves to pasta and tomato dishes, soups and bland fish (and the aforementioned sandwich), but even if you only use it occasionally, brush the leaves every now and then to release its glorious fragrance.

**Sweet Bay** (*Laurus nobilis*) grows well in the UK, although it was originally a Mediterranean shrub. Traditionally, bay is reputed to protect against evil: in the past the death of a bay tree was believed to presage a great disaster. Bay is an evergreen, providing wonderful living colour in the herb garden throughout the year, and can be grown in large pots outside (which helps to keep its size easily controlled). Its fragrance is an intriguing mix of spicy and flowery, very fresh and attractive, although it is necessary to bruise the tough leaves quite hard to release the smell. It grows quite slowly, but can become very large if left to its own devices. The leaves add a delicious flavour to slow-cooking dishes such as stews and casseroles, and can easily be dried in a warm, dry place for ease of storage and use. The dried leaves have a stronger, very slightly different flavour to the fresh, although the fragrance is less intense.

**Chervil** (*Anthriscus cerifolium*) is a very pretty aromatic herb, with attractive, pale green feathery leaves. The fragrance is distinctive and slightly sweet, but quite delicate. Chervil leaves enhance the flavour of other herbs and are often used in 'mixed herb' blends. The leaves should be used fresh, in salads and sauces and to flavour raw vegetables. The plant needs to be kept moist, and will happily grow indoors on a windowsill.

**Chives** (*Allium schoenoprasum*) – those cheerful, hardy relatives of the well-known onion – are a delight in salads, scrambled eggs and mashed potatoes. Their aroma and flavour are milder than that of onions, and they are very easy to grow, both outdoors and on the windowsill, but be sure to keep them watered during dry spells. The flowers look like little purple pompoms and are usually cut and discarded before they set seed, but they are also edible, and can be used to add an unusual decoration to a special salad.

**Dill** (*Anethum graveolens*) is a tall, graceful plant with delicate feathery leaves. The whole herb is delicate in nature and requires a lot of attention, but the piquant, earthy green fragrance and flavour, somehow redolent of country fayres and picnics under the trees, is well worth the effort. The herb is an important ingredient in many fish dishes, especially gravadlax (salmon pressed with dill), and also goes well with vegetables, particularly cucumber and green salad. It is also a very useful addition to goulash and borscht.

**Hyssop** (*Hyssopus officinalis*) is a tall, strongly aromatic shrubby herb, fairly easy to grow and requiring little attention once established. Traditionally hyssop was used for cleansing, and its powerful, slightly minty fragrance creates a wholesome atmosphere in the garden. The leaves can be used for culinary purposes, but the flavour is very intense so the herb should be used with care. It is best enjoyed in the garden, where it will attract bees. Although it can be grown indoors, it will soon outgrow its pot.

**Lemon Balm** (*Melissa officinalis*), although looking somewhat like mint, smells wonderfully of lemons. Try growing it at the side of paths or other places where it will be brushed against and the scent released. In cooking it can be used generously to flavour fish or sweet desserts, and the leaves infused to make a relaxing, calming tea. Lemon balm is extremely easy to grow. Mine simply appeared in the vegetable garden one spring, and has carried on growing happily ever since: transplanting does not seem to bother it. When growing lemon balm for cooking, pinch out the buds before they can flower.

**Marjoram and Oregano** (*Origanum majorana*, *Origanum vulgare*) are different types of the same plant. Marjoram is the milder form, while oregano (or wild marjoram) has a stronger, less delicate flavour and a slightly more pungent perfume. They are low-growing, bushy little plants with woody stems, small leaves and purple flowers that are much loved by bees. The fragrance is quite strong and slightly waxy – very pleasant in the garden. When using in cooking, start off with small amounts and increase according to taste, checking frequently as oregano in particular can overpower more subtle flavours.

**Mint** (*Mentha*) There are several different varieties of mint, each with their own particular fragrance and flavour. They can be very invasive, and are best grown by themselves in a raised bed or large pot.

Spearmint (*Mentha viridis*, *Mentha spicata*) has been highly valued for millennia, in medicines, cosmetics and as a flavouring for food. The ancient Greeks used it to scour their dining tables – it is strongly antiseptic and makes an effective disinfectant – and as a cleansing agent in baths. The Romans, who, like the Egyptians before them, used it to flavour sauces, first introduced it to the UK. Its clean, fresh perfume is a delight in the garden, and it has the added advantage of being a quick and effective breath freshener for when you don't have the time to attend to dental hygiene.

Peppermint (*Mentha piperata*) has a hotter, slightly peppery taste and perfume, and can be something of an acquired taste. An infusion of peppermint leaves in boiling water is effective in settling an upset stomach and alleviating nausea. Be sure to keep spearmint and peppermint plants well apart in the garden to ensure that the flavours remain distinct.

Apple mint (*Mentha rotundifolia*) – sometimes called Bowles mint – has a wonderful aroma, an intriguing mix of apple with an underscent of mint. The leaves can be used to make a fine sauce for lamb dishes and is very tasty with roast pork as well. This is an ideal mint to grow as a decorative herb on the kitchen windowsill: bruise the leaves gently every now and again to fill the room with its fragrance.

Eau de Cologne mint (*Mentha citrata*) smells, as its name suggests, very similar to the refreshing cologne water once used to relieve headaches and cool and freshen hot skin. The fragrance from the plant has a similar effect – try bruising a leaf or two and sniffing the perfume any time you feel a headache threatening. Eau de Cologne mint can be used as a garnish for fruit drinks, but is perhaps most useful as a living air freshener and as an ingredient in *pot pourri*.

Water mint (*Mentha aquatica*), a tall variety with hairy, reddish stems and purple flowers, is a slightly unusual choice of plant for those with a pool in the garden as it grows happily in the wet soil by pool and river banks. Since all mints spread vigorously, it should be kept under control. It is best enjoyed for its fresh, slightly spicy fragrance.

**Parsley** (*Petroselinum crispum*) is perhaps one of the best known herbs in the western world: its high vitamin and iron content have made it extremely popular and desirable as a dietary aid. Its ability to cleanse the breath of the overpowering smell of garlic is well known, and has resulted in many garlic-flavoured foods now having parsley leaves included to lessen the alliaceous odour.

Parsley is reputed only to grow successfully where a woman is the head of the household, and there is a superstition that it should not be transplanted – to do so will bring ill-luck to the gardener. The flavour and fragrance are tangy and tart, and the leaves are used to add flavour to soups, stews and fish dishes. (Unfortunately I loathe the smell of parsley – I would rather endure the scent of garlic!)

**Rosemary** (*Rosmarinus officinalis*) is surrounded by a wealth of tradition. It has a strong association with Christianity: one tradition, calling on its Latin name, refers to it as 'Mary's rose' and links it with Christ's mother. (The Latin actually means 'dew of the sea', reflecting its ability to survive in the salt-spray filled air of the Mediterranean coast.) Another states that the plant will grow no taller than six feet high, since that was how tall Jesus was as an adult and the plant's humility will not permit it to overtop Christ. It is reputed only to thrive in the gardens of the righteous, although my three bushes are growing extremely well, so it might be as well not to be too worried about that tradition! Rosemary improves the memory, and has come to symbolise remembrance, true friendship and faithfulness.

Rosemary grows quite slowly, and left to itself can become very large and sprawling. It is a beautiful plant, with sprays of tiny grey-blue flowers much loved by bees (and moths, if mine are typical of the herb). The leaves are narrow, very dark green above and silvery grey underneath, and the fragrance is unmistakable – a rich, exotic, intense aroma reminiscent of incense. Sprays of rosemary were burned in place of incense in the past. The leaves contain considerable quantities of a slightly waxy, lingering essential oil (try crushing them between your fingers to smell and feel the effect). The herb is evergreen, making it perfect for the fragrant garden in winter.

Rosemary has a host of culinary uses, but it is strongly flavoured so should be used with some care. The dried leaves are perfect for herb pillows and sachets, and are an important ingredient in many *pots pourris*.[7] Best of all, grow it in the garden, place a seat nearby, and simply enjoy the fragrance.

**Sage** (*Salvia officinalis*) is another well-known and much-loved herb. It has been regarded as an all-round healing herb for millennia and throughout the world. In old Arabia it was said 'Why should a man die who grows sage in his garden?' while the equivalent English proverb states 'He who would live for aye,[8] should eat sage in May.' The herb's association with wisdom ('sagacity') echoes its reputation for invigorating the brain and acting as a tonic for the entire body.

It is an attractive, silvery-grey plant with a pungent, warm aroma, slightly bitter to the taste. Often used to counteract the richness and fattiness of dishes such as roast pork or roast duck, the raw leaves can also be added to salads, pickles and cheese, but the flavour is very strong, so use with care. Sage leaves are another important ingredient in *pot pourri*.[4]

**Tarragon** (*Artemisia dracunculus* (French), *Artemisia dracunculoides* (Russian)) is a tall, attractive herb with a distinctive bitter-sweet flavour that is slightly reminiscent of aniseed. The plant is an essential ingredient in many French dishes, and makes an excellent herb vinegar.[9] For culinary purposes, the French variety is preferable as its flavour and fragrance is more delicate. The Russian variety, however, grows taller (up to one-and-a-half metres/four-and-a-half feet) and has a more powerful aroma: grow it against a sunny wall or fence to take advantage of its graceful appearance and exotic perfume.

**Thyme** (*Thymus vulgaris*) is a low-growing herb with tiny leaves and pale purple flowers, ideal for growing at the sides of paths or borders where it can be brushed as people walk past. It is strongly aromatic, and can easily overpower more delicate flavours in cooking, but goes well with dishes cooked with wine.

Lemon thyme (*Thymus citriodorus*) has a milder, lemony flavour and fragrance, pleasant in *pot pourri*[4] and in dishes where thyme would be too strong.

### Herbs for Fragrance

There are a number of herbs that, while traditionally used medicinally, are not ordinarily employed in cooking – these days, at any rate. Many of these are, however, beautifully fragranced and often very attractive, certainly worth considering for the garden.

**Chamomile** (*Anthemis nobilis*) is the best chamomile for the creation of a chamomile lawn since the plant gives off its characteristic, apple-like aroma when crushed. If you do not have the space or resources for an entire lawn, plant some chamomile on a small slope to create a garden 'seat', and make a point of sitting there any time you feel stressed – chamomile is an excellent calming and soothing herb.

**Cowslip** (*Primula veris*), the pretty yellow spring wild flower, has a delicate scent and is very much at home in a wildflower garden or mini-meadow. Since its natural habitats are, like much of the countryside, disappearing fast, growing some in your own garden is a good way to preserve this traditional plant.

**Meadow Sweet** (*Spiraea ulmaria*) is another traditional wild plant that grows happily in a semi-wild garden; in the wild it grows near water and in damp meadows. The plant is beautiful, with dark green leaves and tiny creamy-coloured flowers carried in heavy bunches at the end of tall stems. The flowers have a wonderful, rich vanilla scent, and an infusion made from the leaves is an effective diuretic.

**Rue** (*Ruta graveolens*) has a bitter flavour, and is usually used medicinally rather than in cooking (it is something of an acquired taste). The scent is strong, pungent and quite distinctive. Some people may find it unpleasant, but it forms an interesting contrast to some of the sweeter herbal fragrances.

Rue is a very pretty plant, growing quite tall with silvery, blue-green delicate-looking leaves and small yellow flowers. Be careful when harvesting: the plant's oil may be irritating to some people, especially when picked in full sun after rain. Also be sure to wash your hands thoroughly after picking – or preferably wear gloves as the essential oil is strong and pervasive, and if you forget, five minutes later you will be able to taste the herb in your mouth, even if your hands have been nowhere near your face!

**Pennyroyal** (*Mentha pulegium*), although actually a low-growing, old-fashioned member of the mint family, is used to create a fragrant lawn or to fill in between cracks in paths, more than in cooking, providing a wonderful, refreshing minty smell as you walk in the garden. It is a traditional abortifacient,[10] however, so is best avoided if you are pregnant or trying to conceive.

**Tansy** (*Tanacetum vulgare*) is a fairly common but attractive wild plant, with lovely fern-like leaves and yellow flowers that resemble buttons. It has an intriguing, lemon-camphor fragrance when crushed. Plant the herb around the base of garden seats and the edges of borders, where it can be bruised deliberately to release the aroma.

**Yarrow** (*Achillea millefolium*) is a truly delightful wild flower, with soft, grey-green feathery leaves and pretty white or pinkish flowers. It is usually considered to be a weed, which is a pity, since it is a lovely plant to grow in the garden. Then again, it has been said that a weed is simply a plant growing in the wrong place. Indeed, I would recommend it for all gardens.

Yarrow has a spicy, slightly exotic fragrance. The herb is rich in vitamins and minerals, and the whole plant has many medicinal uses, from easing constipation, water-retention and flatulence, to staunching nosebleeds, helping problem circulation and relieving toothache (chew the leaves). An infusion made by steeping the leaves in boiling water for a few minutes, straining and allowing to cool is an effective toner and freshener for oily skin, or add some to the bathwater to cleanse the skin and relax the body.

Yarrow will spread quite vigorously if left to itself, so some attention is needed to keep it under control. Alternatively, plant the herb in a raised bed to prevent it taking over. It is possible to buy stone, or reconstituted stone, planters designed to fit over manhole covers, thus disguising a somewhat ugly but necessary feature of some gardens: these make ideal homes for the mints or for yarrow.

### A Garden for Living

There may well be occasions when you want to create a garden for a particular purpose – to ease a variety of physical ailments, for example, or to provide a refuge for meditation or inspiration, or as a rich experience for the visually impaired. Visiting other gardens, both National Trust and others that are open to the public as well as friends', may prove useful for generating design ideas, but you are really only limited by your own imagination (and your physical resources, of course). The following are a few suggestions that may help to fire that imagination. Details of the actual plants mentioned may be found in the appropriate chapters.

### An Aromatherapy Garden

To decide which plants to grow, refer to the Table of Essential Oils and Aromatherapy. For example, if you or any member of your household suffer from respiratory problems, include eucalyptus (but do remember it grows very fast and very tall and will require frequent pruning), basil, lavender and peppermint. For stress and nervous complaints, ensure you plant a good quantity of chamomile, and grow rosemary, geranium and roses: hops and yarrow are also useful as calming influences. If you find yourself struggling with weight-related problems, try fennel, rosemary and juniper. Ideally, place your chosen plants in a roughly circular design with a seat of some kind in the centre, so that you may sit surrounded by fragrant and effective natural restoratives.

### The Meditation Garden

Comfort is a primary consideration in a garden such as this. Ensure you have a comfortable seat. A cushioned bench is ideal, or a mossy patch or hummock planted with fragrant chamomile or pennyroyal – see Fragrant Gardens for details – if you intend using low-growing plants as a focus. You will need to decide exactly what sort of design you want, and it is a good idea to sketch it on paper before you start acquiring the plants. Bear in mind that symmetrical shapes (both in the plants you employ and in the basic ground plan itself) aid calm contemplation, while asymmetric designs tend to be more creative and inspirational. Try to fit a regular 'meditation space' into your weekly routine; within a couple of months you will find yourself really looking forward to the time.

You might decide on a simple, Eastern-style design – perhaps one or two fragrantly dramatic plants such as magnolia or peony as a focus for your mind and your eyes, accompanied by wind chimes, a couple of large, intricately weathered rocks, and pale gravel or close-cropped grass as a backdrop.

Water is an excellent focus for meditation. A still pool, quiet fountain or gentle waterfall are all ideal. The mints, violets and violas, and chamomile are ideal for growing around the water source: if possible, grow something fairly simple as a backdrop – tall, graceful ornamental grasses are perfect.

A mandala is a more complicated but nevertheless very effective focus. It will require careful planning – the plants should all be of more or less the same height, and not too quick-growing or the mandala will need so much attention that its contemplative effect will be lost. Contrasting colours (purple and gold, or green and pink) can look stunning, and a spiral design within the main circle will help the mind focus inwards. It is best not to attempt anything too complex or fussy with such a design or the tranquil effect will be lost, but that still leaves scope for plenty of creativity – concentric rings, triangles, a star, a lemniscus,[11] an eye (or an eye of Horus), practically anything can become a focus for meditation, as long as it means something appropriate and special to you, or the person for whom you are creating the garden.

For a creative and inspirational meditation garden, taller, upright shapes, which represent the human spirit reaching upwards, are perhaps more appropriate, as are climbing plants like hops and passionflower (their complex flowers are ideal for sparking new ideas). Bay tree, juniper, even pine if the garden is large enough, are all excellent, as is the corkscrew hazel (*Corylus avellana contorta*). For a touch of the bizarre, include one of the *Euphorbias* (*characias wulfenii* would be perfect), or an *Eryngium* (sea holly) or two. They have no fragrance to speak of, but the shape and colour are quite stunning. If you are feeling particularly adventurous, try planting out your chosen specimens in a mini-maze, so that you are forced to meander as you walk in the garden. It can be a wonderful way of encouraging the mind to explore new ideas.

### A Tactile Garden

This sort of garden is not designed just to please the sense of touch – it should appeal to all the senses, although since it functions as a stimulating or relaxing retreat for the visually impaired, the shape and colour of the chosen plants are perhaps less important than their fragrance and texture.

Any or all of the fragrant flowers and herbs listed in Fragrant Gardens can be employed, but when utilising the lower-growing plants, try placing them in raised beds, so it is not necessary to bend down too far to enjoy their perfume. Group the plants so that the fragrances do not mingle too much, and grow thorny plants such as roses where they won't be accidentally touched or brushed against. Mix fragrant plants with those which are interesting or pleasant to touch – shrubs with contrasting bark, clematis, and lamb's ears (*Stachys*), for example – and try to plant some which have an aural effect: wind blowing through the leaves of birch or willow is a haunting sound, while the dry, papery rustle of empty *Lunaria* seedpods can be quite intriguing. A water feature is also useful when considering sound in such a garden.

**A Mood Garden**
Mood gardens rely to a large extent on colour to reflect or invoke a particular mood or emotion, although shape and texture also play a part.

To invoke passion, choose red-hued plants and flowers (and fruit, if so wished). Roses, the red trunks and branches of dogwood and its fiery red autumnal leaves, purple basil and strawberries are all appropriate.

Blue and violet are cool and contemplative, ideal colours if you intend the garden to be a meditative retreat – lavender, violets, violas, pansies ... For a touch of the exotic, choose silvery-blue plants such as *Lamium*, sage and eucalyptus for a futuristic look, and enhance the space with silver painted ornaments, wind chimes, crystal mobiles, unusual seating, etc. A pool with submerged uplighting in shades of blue, pale purple and white makes a striking centrepiece for night-time parties. With a small fountain operating at the same time, the effect can be dramatic.

White is spiritual and uplifting, beneficial if you spend all day dealing with awkward customers! Night-scented stocks, jasmine and orange blossom are ideal for soothing the stress and tension of a hectic day's work and leaving you ready for a refreshing night's sleep.

Yellow is energising and enlivening, and there are a large number of plants with yellow or yellow-green foliage as well as the best-known fragrant flowers – narcissi for the spring, yellow roses for summer, *Mahonia* for autumn and winter.

Green is soothing and calming, and there are an almost infinite number of shades available in nature. Plant herbs for their fragrance and healing influences, and try to include rosemary and a bay tree, if at all possible.

If you feel so inclined, you could even try a Gothic garden. Plant yew hedges (but make sure no children have access to the berries, which are toxic), rosemary for remembrance, nightshades (*Belladonna*) for their slightly sinister, complex flowers, black or purple pansies for sombre thoughts ...

# 6
# *Feng Shui – a Fragrant Balance*

*Feng shui* (literally 'wind and water') is the physical manifestation of an ancient Chinese philosophy of life that stresses the necessity of balancing the natural, unseen force of life – *Ch'i* – in order to promote health, harmony, happiness and beauty.

*Ch'i* pervades and underpins the entire universe – including, naturally, our human senses! It is perceived as having two forms – *yin*, which is cold, quiet, wet, soft, passive, and *yang*, which is hot, loud, dry, hard and active – which are present in all things in varying proportions. For there to be perfect health and balance, the two need to be in equilibrium. *Ch'i* also has two qualities – *sheng ch'i*, which is positive and constructive, and *sha ch'i*, which is negative and destructive. Naturally enough, it's far better to encourage *sheng ch'i* into your life than to submit to the exigencies of *sha ch'i*!

*Feng shui* can be incorporated into every area of your life: here we will consider the garden. The first principle to be aware of is that a well-tended garden, full of healthy plants, clean fresh water, a mix of colours, shapes, textures and perfumes promotes *sheng ch'i*, while a neglected garden, with rank overgrown vegetation, rough features and stagnant water fosters *sha ch'i*. If you do not have enough time to devote to keeping your dream garden in ideal condition, it might be wise to compromise. Instead of displaying plants that need pruning, staking, mulching and a lot of general care and attention (azaleas, for example), try something more robust and lower maintenance – chrysanthemums, perhaps. If you cannot find the time to keep mowing a large lawn, turn part of it into a wildflower meadow: use native plants and encourage your local bird and insect life, as well as providing a refuge for assorted small animals. (For a really low maintenance garden, see Simplicity Itself, below.)

Generally speaking, in the garden, *yin* is represented by water features, gentle slopes, shadows and shady areas, soft irregular shapes and pastel colours, *yang* by trees, upright rocks, barbecues and garden lights, strong, bright warm colours and angular shapes. However, the Chinese recognise five natural elements (as contrasted with the four more usually encountered in the West) – water, fire, wood, metal and earth (rather than fire, earth, air and water). For true balance, these elements also need to be considered when planning a garden.

**Water** is symbolised, naturally enough, by water features – pools, fountains, streams. Water colours are black or dark blue, its shapes horizontal, wavy or rippling. Its season is winter.

Plants to represent water include irises, watermint, low-growing plants such as gentian, violets and violas, love-in-a-mist (*Nigella*), heather, oregano and thyme.

**Fire** is represented by red or orange flowers, warmly coloured upright stones, candles, garden lights, angular shapes (herringbone patterned patio paving, for example). Its colour is red, its shape triangular and its season summer.

Fire-plants include red, pink and orange-hued roses, red and pink *Astilbe* varieties, carnations, foxgloves (*Digitalis*) and hibiscus. Hyssop – preferably the pink-flowered variety – is an appropriate fire herb.

**Wood** is symbolised, of course, by trees, but also upright features such as wooden posts and tall green plants. Its colour is green, its shape tall, rectangular and upright, and its season is spring.

If you have room for a tree or two, so much the better. For the smaller garden, however, upright plants such as bamboo (if you have the time and energy to keep it under control!), New Zealand flax (*Phormium tenax*), ornamental grasses or reeds (suitable if you have a pool) are most appropriate. Bay tree and rosemary are suitable herbs.

**Metal** colours are white, silver and other metallic colours. Metal's season is autumn, and its shapes domed or curved. In the garden, metallic ornaments, rounded white or silvery grey stones, gravel or light-coloured paving are appropriate.

There are a number of silvery and metallic-looking plants that can be used to symbolise metal in the garden. The best is sage (the ordinary culinary herb, with its silvery blue leaves and pungent fragrance). Others include *Lamium*, lamb's ears (*Stachys lanata*), blue-grey, low-growing ornamental junipers, *Artemisia stelleriana* (a beautiful silvery-grey variety), or any of the silver-grey varieties of sea holly (*Eryngium*).

**Earth** is symbolised by terracotta, clay and bare earth. Its colours are brown, yellow and earthy, its shape is square, and its season early autumn.

In the garden, large pots or planters, raised beds held back with clay or brown ceramic slabs, or terracotta ornaments are ideal. Chrysanthemums, *Sedum* (particularly Autumn Joy), orange and yellow varieties of day lily (*Hemerocallis*), red-hot poker (*Kniphofia*) are appropriate plants to represent earth. Try to grow some bronze fennel, or, even better, red-leaved bergamot (*Monarda didyma*) – bees (and humans!) love its sweet fragrance.

It is usually possible to incorporate at least a few of these suggestions into even a small garden. If you wish to follow *feng shui* principles more strictly, position your metal plants or objects to the west and north-west, a water feature or water-related plants to the north, earth-related plants or features to the north-east and/or south-west, wood to the east and south-east, and fire plants and materials to the south. (A compass is quite important when using *feng shui*!)

A more relaxed method of maintaining equilibrium in the garden would be to ensure that you have a balance of *yin* and *yang* related plants and features.

### *Yin* Correspondences

**Water**. Examples of water features are pools and ponds, fountains, gurgle ponds and wall-mounted waterfalls. Round, octagonal or irregular shapes are best for ponds, and if possible, try to keep a few goldfish, which are excellent for attracting money luck into your life. Ensure you have an uneven number – seven is ideal. The water must be kept clean and clear at all times.

**Shade**. Ferns, moss and shade-loving plants are all appropriate. If the shade is provided by a tree such as a weeping willow, so much the better – trees with drooping branches are very *yin*.

**Low, domed shapes**. Plants that form mounds, or low, smooth rocks, are suitable, as are bushy shrubs.

**Colours and shapes**. All shades of blue, black, green, silver, turquoise and pale purple. Soft, irregular shapes.

**Plants**. Lavender, eucalyptus, honeysuckle, honesty (*Lunaria*), clematis, periwinkle, sage, lilac, lily of the valley, night-scented stocks, miniature *Acer* varieties, weeping willow.

## *Yang* Correspondences

**Light**. Garden lights, candles, shining mobiles, reflective stones or objects positioned in full sun. The barbecue, the midday sun.

**Tall, upright shapes**. Trees, fences, trellises, gazebo or summer house. Rockeries with large, regularly shaped rocks are also appropriate. A rockery with *yin* plants interspersed with *yang* rocks provides a lovely example of equilibrium.

**Colours and shapes**. All shades of red, pink, orange, yellow, gold. Hard, solid, geometric shapes.

**Plants**. Roses, *Mahonia*, hyacinths, peony, poppies, stocks, bay tree, coniferous trees.

There are several plants which are, traditionally, particularly beneficial, although not all of them will grow in all gardens. A peach tree promotes health and longevity, while a cherry tree brings health and happiness, particularly to women. Bamboo symbolises a long, healthy life, as do coniferous trees. Peonies are reputed to bring strength and stamina, particularly for men. And chrysanthemums bring happiness into the home: try planting some gold-coloured chrysanthemums outside the front door so that their *ch'i* may enter each time the door is opened.

## *Feng Shui* Scents

*Yin* fragrances are generally sweet and floral (for example, jasmine), while *yang* are pungent and aromatic (for example, sage), as befits their fundamental character. However, each of the five elements also has an associated scent. These correspondences are designed for the house[1] rather than the garden due to the difficulty of growing some of the herbs in temperate climates. Use them in fragrancers to emphasise the qualities of the desired elements.

**Water** – 'green' fragrances: herbs such as basil, chamomile, peppermint, oregano, thyme.

**Fire** – spicy fragrances: ginger, cardamom, cumin, cloves.

**Wood** – cedarwood, sandalwood, cypress.

**Metal** – citrus fragrances: grapefruit, lemon, orange.

**Earth** – resinous: frankincense, myrrh, eucalyptus.

*Feng Shui* **Fragrance in the Home**

In the traditional Compass School of *feng shui*, the eight main points of the compass represent different facets of life, and can be superimposed over a ground plan of the home to indicate which rooms influence particular spheres of activity, as follows:

**North** – your career or vocation, progress. (Water element.)

**North-east** – education, wisdom, knowledge, enlightenment. (Earth element.)

**East** – your family, your health, children. (Wood element.)

**South-east** – money, wealth, prosperity, your possessions. (Wood element.)

**South** – fame, recognition, publicity. (Fire element.)

**South-west** – relationships, happiness, contentment. (Earth element.)

**West** – creativity, leisure and pleasure, fertility. (Metal element.)

**North-west** – new beginnings, travel, helpful people. (Metal element.)

If, for example, your career could do with a boost, try adding some 'water' essential oils (basil or peppermint, perhaps) to a fragrancer in whichever room faces north in your home. If you are worried about the health of a family member, use a 'wood' essential oil – sandalwood is excellent in cases of ill health[2] – in an east-facing room, and place a photograph or small personal possession of the ailing person behind the diffuser, or underneath it if it is safe and possible to do so. A little sympathetic magic can be highly effective in these operations.

A little thought will suggest a host of other ideas for enhancing and balancing your life and domestic environment. Experiment and see what suits you best.

## Simplicity Itself

For the lowest of all low-maintenance gardens, pave over or cover the available space with a deep layer of chippings. Find five appropriate containers and place in them five appropriate plants from the suggestions above, then position them in a rough circle. Ideally, place a simple feature – a birdbath or other water-related article, or an interesting rock – in the centre. The result can look stunning, and requires practically no work to keep it looking good.

# 7
# *Fragrant Foods*

Eating is one of life's great pleasures. Of course, it is also essential for the preservation and continuance of life itself, like breathing and breeding (which can also be considerable pleasures in themselves!), but the possibilities for new gustatory experiences are almost endless – as evidenced by the never-ending supply of new cookery books ...

The smell of just about any edible substance is appealing to a hungry person – saliva fills the mouth and the stomach may start rumbling in anticipation and preparation for the process of eating food. Initially, eating was simply a matter of providing sustenance for the body. However, as the human race became more 'civilised', food began to assume more importance – not just in the amount provided, but in the variety of foodstuff presented (and sometimes the ulterior motive).

The consumption of food is, traditionally, very much a communal act. Rulers and aristocrats vied with each other over the size and sumptuousness of their banquets: tribal chiefs proclaimed their wealth and status by the physical size of their wives (only a wealthy man could afford to keep a large woman). Festivals were – and frequently still are – celebrated with a feast, and it is still common practice to take a prospective romantic partner out for a meal in the very early days of courtship. Business is discussed over lunch; meeting for coffee and cakes is a simple, regular pleasure between friends; hot summer days are commemorated with picnics and barbecues, and children's birthdays usually include some kind of edible celebration, even if only a birthday cake. Over the years, eating has become associated with having a good time!

These days, the pace of modern life has meant that many people no longer have the time (or the culinary skills) to enjoy the experience of freshly made, home cooked food as convenience foods in front of the TV or at the desk have, to a large extent, taken over from the family meals of the past. However, it is still possible to enjoy something of the more leisurely meals of the past – by using herbs, aromatic spices, and fragrant flowers to enhance the flavours of food.

## Herbs and Spices

The use of herbs in medicine and for flavouring food has been evident throughout history on a global scale. No matter where the local population lived, there was always some sort of green, flavoursome herb growing in the vicinity, even if the choice was fairly limited in some of the less hospitable areas of the earth. Spices, however, are a slightly different story. Most of the spices with which we are familiar today are natives of the tropical and sub-tropical zones, and were not widely available in Europe until the late Middle Ages (from the end of the 14th century: the Middle Ages lasted from around the middle of the 11th century until the end of the 15th) although they had been imported into Rome for millennia[1] and have always been in widespread use in Middle Eastern countries. Until that time, mustard seed was really the only spice available to the general public in Europe, anything else being well beyond their means.

From the end of the 14th century until the early days of the 17th, spices were used quite heavily – by those who could afford them. Since most had to be imported from a considerable distance, they were extremely expensive and therefore frequently used as status symbols. Pepper, for example, was literally worth its weight in gold. Spices were kept locked away in specially made cabinets and were often the most costly item in the household accounts. However, it was also possible to buy sauces made by professional sauce-makers, who ran a profitable business selling to households wishing to impress friends and family.

Food tended to be heavily flavoured, especially in wealthy households. A favourite sauce of the time was *cameline*, a concoction of cloves, cinnamon, mace, nutmeg, ginger, grains of paradise,[2] long pepper,[3] and vinegar-soaked bread. (I have to confess I've never tried it, but it sounds interesting ...) Sweet and sour dishes were also very popular, made simply with sugar and vinegar, and the sweeter spices – cinnamon, nutmeg, saffron, ginger – were used extensively in baked dishes, cakes and desserts. It is not overly surprising that the most highly desired beauty feature of the time was a full set of undecayed teeth!

From the beginning of the 17th century, as trade increased and more luxury goods were imported, the cost of spices dropped. Accordingly, they became less of a status symbol, and were not used so ostentatiously – certainly by the wealthy. New spices were available; allspice, vanilla and the various spices derived from the *Capsicum* (chilli, paprika, cayenne) were imported from America, along with new vegetable foods – potatoes, yams, tomatoes, maize, and, of course (and to the eternal thanks of chocoholics everywhere), cocoa.

These days an enormous variety of spices can be found in every supermarket, not just as individual spices, but also in blends, in powder or paste form: Chinese five-spice powder, Thai seven-spice mix, English pudding spice, Cajun seasoning, all the Indian blends from balti to masala ... There is really no excuse (apart from an allergy to any of the ingredients) for anyone not to explore culinary delights from around the world. They are a treat for the nose as well as the tastebuds.

**Allspice** (*Pimenta dioica*), native to Jamaica, has a spicy, warm, almost floral aroma – an ideal addition to woody or winter *pot pourri* – and a peppery, clove-like taste. Allspice is an important ingredient in carrot and apple cakes, and improves the flavour of rice dishes. A small pinch in a stew or casserole helps to intensify the taste of other flavourings.

**Cardamom** (*Elettaria cardamomum*) is native to India and Sri Lanka where it is cultivated high up in the mountains. It is a very ancient spice, having been in use in India for millennia, and is one of the more expensive. The fragrance is warm and distinctive, with a pungent note, and the taste bitter, lingering and strong, but nevertheless refreshing. Cardamom is used in both sweet and savoury dishes, and added to coffee in the Middle East. Medicinally, the spice is used as a remedy for stomach problems.

**Caraway** (*Carum carvi*), native to Europe and a member of the same herb family as parsley, has a warm, slightly bitter fragrance and taste. Caraway imparts a hint of lemon when combined with other vegetables and fruit, and the seeds add flavour to bread, cheese and cabbage. Medicinally, caraway eases indigestion.

**Cinnamon** (*Cinnamomum verum*), native to Sri Lanka, is the dried bark of a variety of laurel. Its sweet, slightly woody and very distinctive aroma and flavour has been used in cakes and breads in Europe since at least the 15th century. It goes particularly well with chocolate, pears, rice dishes and lamb. (It is often used in Middle Eastern savoury dishes.) Powdered cinnamon is a useful ingredient in *pot pourri*, and is a warming spice to add to hot drinks to ease colds and flu.

**Cloves** (*Eugenia aromatica*) are the unopened flower buds of the shrub, native to the Moluccas. Another ancient, valuable and esteemed spice, cloves have a rich, deep, distinctive and long-lasting aroma that makes them ideal for use in *pot pourri*. The flavour is extremely sharp and bitter, and biting on raw cloves numbs the mouth. (Clove oil is a tried and trusted remedy for toothache – only for the pain, though: a visit to the dentist is still necessary to resolve the cause of the problem.)

**Coriander** (*Coriandrum sativum*), indigenous to the Mediterranean, has been used as a culinary and medicinal herb for both its fruit and its leaves. The spice is obtained from the seeds, which smell and taste completely different from the leaves. Coriander seeds (whole and powdered) have a wonderful fragrance, partly sweet, partly spicy and peppery, with a hint of wood and a faint tang of oranges. Coriander has been used in both sweet and savoury dishes the world over, and is an essential spice in curries. Medically, coriander, and especially its essential oil, are constituents in migraine and indigestion medicines.

**Cumin** (*Cuminum cyminum*) originated in the Nile valley, but rapidly spread to other parts of the world – India, North Africa, the Middle Eastern countries and China. From Spain it was exported to South America. Cumin has a strong, intense aroma which is highly distinctive, and a sharp, hot, lingering flavour. A pinch of cumin deepens the flavour of most savoury dishes. Medicinally, it is used in India as a remedy for diarrhoea and indigestion.

**Fenugreek** (*Trigonella foenum-graecum*), native to the eastern Mediterranean, has a unique and memorable aroma – spicy, grassy and somewhat exotic. The flavour is similar, and the spice should be used with some care, as it is very strong and will dominate other ingredients. It adds an interesting element to *pot pourri*. Medicinally, fenugreek is a source of diosgenin, used in the production of oral contraceptives.

**Ginger** (*Zingiber officinale*) has been cultivated in Asiatic countries for thousands of years. The spice is an excellent aid to digestion, and can be added to hot drinks in cases of cold and flu – it has a warming effect, and may help to promote perspiration and improve the circulation. The spice is obtained from the rhizome (the root-like, horizontal underground stem), which can be sliced, dried, powdered, crushed, grated, candied or preserved. The aroma of ginger is sharp, spicy and invigorating: the flavour hot and lingering. It is best not eaten fresh and raw if you are not used to it – the effect feels a little like burning the inside of your mouth!

**Juniper** (*Juniperus communis*) berries are perhaps best known as the flavouring for gin, and they do smell pleasantly like the alcoholic drink, with a bitter-sweet undertone. Their flavour is sweetish, but with a hint of pine – intriguing, but something of an acquired taste.

**Mace** (*Myristica fragrans*) is the outer covering (aril) of the nutmeg seed, the fruit of the evergreen tree native to the Moluccas. It has a rich, warm fragrance and slightly bitter flavour, and although it can be used in sweet recipes, it is generally added to savoury dishes.

**Nutmeg** (*Myristica fragrans*) is the kernel of the nutmeg seed. Nutmeg has a wonderfully distinctive, warm, sweetish aroma and a unique flavour: an essential ingredient in potato-based soups and pumpkin dishes. It blends well with honey, and is often used in rich baked-goods and cakes.

**Paprika**, one of the spices produced from the chilli pepper (*Capsicum annuum*), has a warm, terracotta-red colour and a sweetish, oddly dry aroma, which adds an unusual but pleasing note to a spicy *pot pourri*. Paprika is widely used in Hungarian, Spanish and Balkan dishes: it has a bittersweet flavour.

**Saffron** (*Crocus sativus*) is the most expensive spice in the world. It takes over 20,000 of the dried, golden stigmas of the saffron crocus to produce just 4 ounces/125g of saffron – and they can only be picked by hand. Saffron has a distinctive, memorable and long-lasting fragrance and a bitter, spicy taste. It is rich in vitamin B2 and riboflavin, and is used in Indian medical preparations for digestive and urinary tract problems.

**Star Anise** (*Illicium verum*) is the fruit of an evergreen tree of the magnolia family, native to the South of China. The seed is pretty, resembling an eight-pointed star, and smells strongly of liquorice, with a distinctive sweet note. It makes a very attractive addition to a *pot pourri*, especially if laid on the top of the mix, where its shape can be clearly seen. It is one of the ingredients of five-spice powder, and is used medicinally as a remedy for colic and rheumatism.

**Turmeric** (*Curcuma longa*), native to India, smells fresh and spicy, with a hint of citrus. The flavour is bitter and slightly musky, an essential ingredient in many curry blends. Used as a dye, it produces a bright, golden yellow colour. Medicinally, it is used in the East for liver ailments.

**Vanilla** (*Vanilla planifolia*) is native to Central America, and was used for centuries by the Aztecs as a food flavouring. Ground vanilla was added to the chocolate beverage drunk by the Aztec emperor Montezuma. The pods grow on the vanilla vine, and require a lengthy and complex curing process before they can be used commercially, which may explain the high cost of real vanilla. Synthetic vanilla has been available since 1847 and provides around 90% of the flavour now needed for commercial purposes. It is worthwhile buying just one pod and keeping it in the sugar jar: it will last for years and impart a delicious vanilla flavour and fragrance to the sugar.

Most of the more usual herbs have been investigated in Chapter 5, Gardens, but lemongrass was not included, because it is not really practicable to try growing it in a temperate zone unless you can provide the correct conditions. However, you might have some success with it as a houseplant for it grows well in hot, sunny conditions with moderate watering. But it does spread quickly, so use a large pot.

Native to South-East Asia, lemongrass has become well-known in the West with the advent of interest in Thai and Indonesian cooking. It has a fresh, clean fragrance, distinctly lemon-like, but not exactly the same. To experience the difference, try sniffing freshly sliced lemongrass and comparing it with a slice of fresh lemon. In cooking, use fresh, cut into slices, or in powder form (use the latter sparingly).

## Flowers

The idea of eating flowers may sound a little strange, but it has been done for millennia – there are Chinese recipes using flowers dating back around five thousand years. In fact, it's actually something most of us do, at least some of the time. Broccoli, calabrese, cauliflower and artichokes are the flowers of their respective plants; the confection known as Turkish delight was originally flavoured with attar of roses (rose essential oil); elderflower cordial (mixed with still or sparkling water) is a delicious and refreshing summer drink – neglected for decades but now becoming well-known again, and crystallised rose petals and violets are still used to decorate special-occasion cakes. There are, however, a much greater variety of flowers[4] that can be used to give colour and flavour to salads, soups, sauces and deserts.

### Carnations and Pinks
The clove-flavoured and perfumed petals of carnations and pinks add a definite hint of the unusual to salads, but use sparingly. They can also be added to home-made pickles for that exotic touch!

### Elderflowers
The large, flat flowerheads of elderflowers make delicious and wonderfully perfumed fritters. Dip the freshly picked, well-washed flowerheads in a light batter and fry lightly in very hot butter or oil for about a minute, dust very lightly with fine caster sugar, or add a squeeze of lemon juice (or both) and enjoy …

### Lavender
Add a sprig of lavender to a small airtight jar of caster sugar. The lavender will flavour and perfume the sugar, making an interesting addition to desserts, cakes and hot puddings. Try sprinkling a little on pancakes for an unusual light meal.

### Marigolds

Marigolds, with their citrus-like perfume and flavour, make a very attractive addition to a salad as the bright golden petals contrast beautifully with green leaves. Marigolds are also an intriguing addition to desserts. They can be added to *consommé*, or chicken soup: cut the petals of two or three marigold flowers into very small pieces and simmer for five minutes in a little water over a fairly high heat. Use the water and petals as a base for the soup.

### Nasturtium

Perhaps the best known of edible flowers are nasturtiums. These flamboyant, robust, red, yellow and orange trailing plants seem to have a special place in gardeners' hearts, and are much loved by children. (They are extremely quick and easy to grow.) They are also delicious: both the leaves and the flowers have a hot, peppery-spicy flavour and fragrance when chopped, and nasturtium seeds can be used as a cheaper alternative to capers in home-made tartare sauce. The flowers can be used whole as a very attractive garnish to a green salad, while the leaves can be added to a salad or eaten in sandwiches with cold meats.

### Primrose and Cowslip

The flowers of primrose and cowslip were traditionally used as decorations for cakes – especially for Mothering Sunday. They are best used crystallised (see below) on cakes, or fresh as an intriguing and subtly flavoured garnish for crêpes, pancakes or salads.

### Roses

For a really unusual accompaniment to cold meats, try pickling rosebuds! Pick the smallest rosebuds, wash thoroughly and place in a jar. Heat white wine vinegar to boiling and add sugar to taste, then cool and pour into the jar. Seal and store in a cool, dark place, and leave for several weeks before use.

It is also possible to make rose petal jam. Gather and weigh a good quantity of red rose petals: you will need the same weight of sugar. Snip off any white parts of the petals, place in a preserving pan with the sugar and a very little water and heat gently until the sugar has dissolved, then boil the liquid until a little of the jam sets when dropped onto a cold plate. Pour into warmed jars, seal and allow to cool.

**Rosehips**
Rosehip and apple jelly makes an interesting accompaniment to hot pork or poultry dishes. Use tart cooking apples, and half their weight of rosehips. Wash and roughly chop the apples and bring to the boil in a large saucepan with enough water to cover them. Simmer until the apples turn to pulp. Wash and finely chop the rosehips, add to the apples and cook for another fifteen minutes, then strain overnight through a fine sieve or coarse muslin cloth. Measure the resultant liquid, place in a preserving pan, and add 1lb/500g of sugar for each 1 pint/½ litre of the apple and rosehip juice. Heat gently until the sugar has dissolved, then boil until a little of the jelly sets when dropped onto a cold plate. Seal in warmed jars and allow to cool before use.

**Violets**
An unusual and delicately fragranced soup can be made using violets. Cook 2oz/50g of long grain white rice in 1¾ pints/1 litre of light, preferably vegetable stock. When the rice is soft, add a cup of fresh violets and simmer very gently for a couple of minutes. Serve immediately.

**Crystallised Flowers**
Use freshly gathered violets, violas, rose petals, primroses, cowslips, pansies, carnations or pinks, making sure the flowers are undamaged. Whisk the white of an egg gently, stopping before it becomes frothy, and either dip the flowers or petals into the white or – if you have the time and patience – paint the white over the flowers or petals. Dip the flowers or petals into caster sugar, ensuring they are completely covered, then shake off the surplus and leave the flowers to dry on greaseproof paper (in a warm room is best). When they have hardened, they can be stored in an airtight container for about a week in a cool place.

Crystallised flowers make charming, old-fashioned decorations for home-made cakes and sweets, especially when on presents for loved ones, and have the added benefit of showing how much care and thought has been put into the gift.

## Flower Waters

The most well-known are rose water and orange water: if you do not want (or do not have the resources) to make your own, both are easily available commercially and smell wonderfully of their respective plants, although they are mostly made from synthetic ingredients these days. Perhaps the easiest way to enjoy their flavour and fragrance is to make up rose or orange syrup. Heat the flower water gently with caster sugar until you have the right consistency and use on desserts: rose flavoured syrup in particular is essential with *gulab jaman* (a delicious but highly calorific Indian dessert of deep-fried milk and spice balls). Both syrups are excellent on crêpes and pancakes.

## Teas and Tisanes

The black, fragrant leaves that are familiar to almost everyone as tea come from the *Camellia sinensis*, actually an evergreen tree that is trained to grow as a bush. Originally from China, the bush is now grown in many sub-tropical areas of the world. The bush takes three to five years to grow to three or four feet/one metre high, the right height and maturity for the leaves to be easily harvested and processed into the familiar and much-loved beverage.

The top bud and the first two leaves are the parts usually picked. The leaves are initially spread loosely onto trays in darkened rooms, and left for about eight hours to begin drying. At that stage they are soft and flexible, easy to cut and roll by machine. The prepared leaves are then dried in ovens to preserve the flavour.

The leaves are then carefully classified by an experienced grader, packed (either into teabags or as loose tea), packaged and delivered.

A tisane is a herbal tea. Used both as a gentle, caffeine-free alternative to normal tea or coffee, and as a remedy for a variety of common ailments, tisanes have been used for centuries – if not millennia – and are easy to prepare at home. If you have the resources to grow and dry your own herbs, so much the better – you can be sure they are not treated with any kind of insecticide or other chemical. Herbs can be most easily dried on racks. Tying them in bunches and hanging up to dry looks attractive, but can lengthen the time required and can lead to the sprays in the middle of the bunch developing mould. If you have no alternative, tie the herbs loosely, with no more than eight stems of sprays in any one bunch, keep the individual herbs separate, and check frequently to ensure the entire bunch is drying properly.

Make sure there is plenty of space between the herbs for air to circulate, and leave to dry somewhere warm and shaded – an airing cupboard is ideal. When the herbs have dried, strip the leaves and flowers from the stems and store in airtight, preferably tinted glass bottles, in a cool place and out of the light.

As a general guideline, use one teaspoon of dried herbs, or three teaspoons of fresh herbs, per mug and keep covered while the tea is steeping. If making a pot of the tea, use one tablespoon of dried herbs or three of fresh. Use boiling water and allow to steep for a minute of two, depending on how strong you like the tea, and sweeten with honey if absolutely necessary. The smell alone is enough to revive tired and jaded spirits!

**Useful Tisanes**

For relaxation, or to relieve insomnia, try making your own chamomile tea – use the dried or fresh flowers (in the quantities noted above) and drink before retiring for the night. For a slightly different fragrance and flavour, use equal parts chamomile and lemon balm.

As a general tonic, to relieve uncomfortable but non-urgent stomach complaints and nausea, or to help ease the suffering accompanying a head cold, make a mint tisane (peppermint is recommended). Peppermint tea also clears the mind and leaves the mouth feeling fresh and ready for action!

To alleviate water retention, try dandelion tea. This tisane is also a useful tonic, and may help to ease some of the discomfort associated with rheumatism. Parsley herbal tea is also reputed to help rheumatism.

Elderflower tea is an excellent remedy for colds, and can help soothe asthma. (Of course, asthma requires medical treatment in the first instance, but the tisane is soothing and comforting, aiding recovery after an attack.) The tea also provides warming relief from chills.

**Flower and Fruit Teas**
Drunk as an alternative to Indian or China tea, floral teas are refreshing and fragrant. There are many commercially available today: try jasmine (famous as an aphrodisiac and antidepressant) for instant stimulation, or rose pouchong for relaxation – it really does smell and taste of rose petals. Try some of the fruit teas – grapefruit or lemon for a quick, vibrant lift, and forest fruits or honey and ginseng for stamina. Experiment: many supermarkets and specialist shops sell individual teabags, so you can try the teas before you buy a packet.

**Herb Vinegars**
Ideally, use clear vinegar – or, even better, cider or wine vinegar. Fill a large-necked jar or bottle with the vinegar, and add the crushed leaves of your chosen herb(s). Tarragon, basil, rosemary, chives, mint, thyme and even garlic cloves and peppercorns can be used for flavour. Leave to infuse for a couple of weeks on a sunny (but not hot) windowsill, turning every now and then. Strain the vinegar into a chosen bottle – there are a variety of attractive, empty glass bottles available. These vinegars make thoughtful gifts for culinary-minded friends – and add a fresh stem or spray of the principal herb as a 'label'.

Use the same method to make bottles of flavoured oils – use sunflower or light olive oil (the latter will have a stronger taste but is better for the liver), and try experimenting with different herbs or herb mixes.

**Wines**
Wines of various types have been made throughout the world for millennia – the art and skill of making wine is very ancient. It is also surprisingly easy to practise in your own home.

Some basic equipment is needed – fermentation jars (usually glass and known as demijohns) and airlocks, plastic tubing for siphoning, a large funnel, wine bottles and corks. A corking tool is also useful, though not essential – a hammer will serve the same purpose, although it requires more care. Some method for clearing and/or filtering the wine is also advisable, but once acquired it will last for a very long time. Hygiene is vitally important to the wine-making process – all equipment must be sterilised before use. Sterilising again afterwards, before storing, is a good habit, too. Sodium metabisulphite (most conveniently bought in pill form as Campden tablets) is the most usual sterilising agent, but use with great caution if you suffer from asthma, since the fumes from dissolving Campden tablets have been known to trigger an attack. A warm, not hot, place where the fermentation vessel can sit, undisturbed, for the time it takes for the wine to ferment is also essential. The fermentation time can vary from a couple of months to a couple of years, depending on what sort of wine you intend making (and how long you can resist the temptation to drink it!)

It is possible to make wine from almost any edible ingredient, including such vegetables as potatoes, peapods and parsnips; rice, tea (I make a fine coffee wine, which, as well as tasting and smelling quite wonderful, has the interesting quality of thoroughly inebriating the drinker while keeping them extremely awake and alert at the same time[5] ... blame the caffeine!), most fruit, and a number of different flowers – including several usually considered to be weeds.

The main component of wine is, naturally, water. Sugar, wine yeast, tannin (to increase the flavour as wine made without tannin is often insipid), and the ingredients to actually create your chosen wine are also required. A large number of home-made wine recipes call for sultanas or raisins, to provide the basic fruit for the wine, but it is possible to buy cans of prepared concentrated grape juice (red, white or rosé) for use as a shortcut. Wine yeast is readily available from chemists or specialist home-brew shops, and the instructions for use are usually written on the tub or packet. For wine of a higher than usual alcoholic strength, try using sherry or port-style yeast.

There are innumerable books available giving full instructions on how to make different sorts of wine. (If you are using canned grape juice, the instructions are very often printed on the box.) Here, I shall only make some suggestions as to a few of the more interesting or unusual ingredients that can be added to the basic wine must (the mix of fruit or fruit juice, water, sugar and yeast that actually creates the wine). The juice and zest of an orange and a lemon should be added to each of the following recipe suggestions – and it is very important, when using your own ingredients, to ensure they have not been sprayed with any kind of insecticide or weedkiller – all ingredients should be thoroughly washed before use, in any case. The amounts given here refer to dry measurements – the flowers should be placed in a measuring jug and pressed down lightly. When preparing flowers for use in wine, place them in a scrupulously clean pail and cover with near-boiling water, then allow to stand for three days, stirring every day, before straining and adding to the fermentation vessel. Each recipe will make a gallon of wine.

### Carnation Wine

Make sure you use the scented variety. Carnation wine requires half a gallon/2½ litres of preferably red carnation flowers, and white grape juice, or 6oz/170g of sultanas. This makes a medium, beautifully scented wine to warm the first days of autumn.

### Clover Wine

Use pink clover flowers (half a gallon/2½ litres), two each of oranges and lemons, and a medium piece of ginger root, bruised. It is recommended that you boil the citrus juices, sugar and flowers in a pan before pouring into the pail. Use only a little white grape juice or sultanas, if any at all. This recipe requires a little pectin-destroying enzyme – follow the accompanying instructions – added to the pail after the hot water has cooled down and before straining in order to ensure the resultant wine is clear, not cloudy.

### Coltsfoot Wine

It is possible to buy coltsfoot flowers from home-brew shops for this recipe, if you cannot find any growing wild. They make a light, dry, delicately fragranced wine. The recipe is identical to that for dandelion (see below).

### Dandelion Wine

If you have ever despaired over what to do with the dandelions in the lawn, try this recipe. It uses the flowers before they set seed, thus preventing their spreading further. But make sure the plants have not been sprayed with any chemicals. The recipe makes a wonderful, pale golden, summery wine with a unique, intriguing fragrance.

Use ¾ gallon/3 ½ litres of fresh dandelion flowers and a medium piece of bruised ginger root. Boil for half an hour in a large pan with sugar and the citrus juices. When straining, squeeze the dandelion flowers against the side of the pail to extract all their essence. This wine does not require any grape juice or fruit, but you will need to add a little pectin-destroying enzyme to the pail.

### Elderflower Wine

Whatever your opinion of the smell of elderflowers, they make a truly delicious, light golden, robust country wine – as do the later berries, of course. Use ¾ gallon/3 ½ litres of fresh elderflowers. It is not necessary to strip them from the flat flower heads – leave them to infuse as they are and strain them later. Follow the recipe for dandelion wine (above) but do not add any pectin-destroying enzyme.

### Honeysuckle Wine

Since this recipe requires two pints of honeysuckle flowers, it's only practicable if you have easy access to a lot of honeysuckle. Use only a little grape juice or about 4oz/113g of raisins. Cover the flowers, citrus juice and zest with hot water, add a crushed Campden tablet, stir and leave to stand for 24 hours, then add dissolved sugar and the yeast and leave to stand for a further week before straining into the fermentation vessel.

The wine tastes of honeysuckle, and is a wonderfully special drink for honeymoons …

### Marigold Wine

Use ¾ gallon/3 ½ litres of marigold flowerheads, and the juice and zest of two lemons. This makes a pleasant, medium wine with a pretty yellow-orange colour.

### Rose Wine

Probably the ultimate drink for lovers of all ages! Whether drunk in the garden on warm summer evenings or in front of the fire on cold winter nights, rose wine smells and tastes of roses, and is very special whatever the season – or reason.

Use a minimum of 4 pints/2⅓ litres of strongly perfumed rose petals – red are best – and 6oz/170g of sultanas. It is worth while using the real fruit in this recipe; chop the sultanas up small before adding to the pail. Ensure you leave the must to stand for a week before straining into the fermentation vessel. Try not to drink too soon!

### Mead

Although it is not produced from flowers, mead is made from honey, which is itself a floral end product of sorts. Home-made mead is a delightful golden colour with an intense, intoxicating honey fragrance, intensely sweet and rich.

Dissolve 3 pounds/1⅖ kilos of your favourite honey in warm – not hot – water, add the juice of one orange and one lemon, a quarter of a teaspoon of grape tannin powder, and the prepared yeast. Then leave to ferment for as long as you can (at least four months). Bottled and labelled attractively, this makes a perfect gift for newly-weds ...

# 8
# *Perfumes*

There is no doubt about it – the perfume industry is very big business indeed. Worth literally billions worldwide, perfumes figure largely on present lists for all sorts of occasions – birthdays, Christmas, anniversaries ... There is a huge variety to choose from, from big name, hugely expensive designer fragrances to the humbler, but no less enchanting and very much cheaper eco-friendly perfumes now produced by 'green' cosmetic companies.

The art (and science) of creating a fragrance is a complex one, and top perfumers occupy a very special and prestigious niche in the commercial world. It can take two years or more, and hundreds of ingredients, both natural and synthetic, to design and create a new perfume, but the rewards can be enormous. And the recipes are, of course, kept very, very secret ...

Why do we use perfumes? Why do we try to overlay our own, unique, individual personal scent with something someone else has devised?

There are a variety of reasons. Diminishing (or disguising) unpleasant body odour is one of the more civil, especially for those working in a hot, hectic environment where there are many people in a small area. In a busy office or the floor of the stock market, for example, the smell of sweat – and especially stale sweat – is an unwelcome, if not necessarily consciously recognised, distraction. Using deodorant and some sort of pleasant smelling fragrance shows consideration for others, and minimises personal embarrassment.[1] It may also help to lessen the impact of pheromones.

From medieval times onwards, perfumes of various types, from flower waters and fragrant lotions for the body, to scented posies and pomanders to carry, were employed (though mainly by the wealthy) to disguise the rank smells of unwashed bodies, rotting rubbish and raw sewage that were an unwelcome side effect of living in larger towns and cities. Later, of course, they were also used simply because people liked them.

Perfume can be a status symbol. Long-lasting, complex fragrances are surprisingly noticeable, and the more complex the perfume the more it costs. Wearing an expensive fragrance announces to all and sundry that you have money – or are considered valuable by someone else who has money …

Of course, some people wear perfume simply because it appeals to them and evokes some kind of emotion or feeling. Adding a drop of a musky, seductive fragrance before going out for a meal with someone you find attractive, or wearing something crisp, fresh and business-like to impress others with your no-nonsense, efficient attitude at work, are just two examples. Fragrance lends itself naturally to enabling the wearer to portray a particular element of their character, either a real trait or one that they would like to be real. The beauty of perfume is that if it makes you feel beautiful, desirable, efficient, tender etc., etc., 95% of the time your brain will perform all the right actions, and produce all the right responses, to make it true (within reason, of course).

Perfumes have been used since time immemorial, and in every part of the world. By wearing a fragrance, even something as simple and venerable as a splash of lavender water, we participate in an activity that is almost as old as the human race.

### Defining Fragrances

Throughout history, various people have tried to define different families of smells. Perhaps the earliest was Plato, who simply divided smells into 'pleasant' and 'unpleasant'. This, of course, is open to much debate, as smells that some people find unpleasant may be extremely pleasant to others. Carl von Linné (1707–78) introduced a sevenfold system – aromatic, fragrant, ambrosial (musky), alliaceous (garlic-like), hircine (goaty), repulsive, and nauseous. At the beginning of the 20th century, Hendrick Zwaardemaker added two further categories – ethereal (fruit and wine) and empyreumatic (creosote and roasted coffee – not together, of course!) – and to some extent, most common fragrances fit into these classifications, although it would be difficult to define strictly which smells would fall into the repulsive and nauseous categories.

In the aromatherapic garden, a different system of classification is used. The five 'fragrance families' are: citrus (orange, lemon, grapefruit), floral (rose, jasmine, lavender, etc.), green ('herby' scents – basil, thyme, peppermint, rosemary), spicy (fennel, juniper, bay), and woody or balsamic (birch, yarrow, cedar).

Commercial perfumers employ a complex and sophisticated array of fragrance types, divided in the first instance into three, four, or even five 'families', and then into further more specific subdivisions. Of course, there is bound to be some overlap between the subdivisions when dealing with something as powerful and subtle as fragrance – and not everyone agrees on which families the various fragrances should be allocated to in the first place. However, the following may serve to give some insight into the fascinating, complicated world of perfume.

The first, and perhaps most popular family, is the florals. This includes such ancient favourites as rose, jasmine, violet, orange blossom, gardenia and lily of the valley (these last two do not contain essential oils, and their fragrances are most usually recreated by synthetic means for the perfume industry).

The second family is *chypre* (pronounced SHE prr: French for Cyprus). *Chypre* perfumes include the citrus fragrances, bergamot and oakmoss.

The third is the oriental. This covers spicy perfumes such as carnation, cinnamon, the resins – myrrh, frankincense and gum benzoin, vanilla and balsamic scents – and 'animal' fragrances such as musk and civet (or, hopefully, their synthetic counterparts).

A commonly accepted fourth family is the *fougère* (French for fern) group, sometimes referred to as 'green'. This includes the herbal fragrances – basil, bay, rosemary – along with vetivert and lavender.

A final family, although it is sometimes included with the orientals, is woody. This includes sandalwood, cedar, pine and cypress.

The floral family is usually subdivided into fresh (which overlaps slightly with the *fougère* family), pure floral, aldehydic (fruity – apple or strawberry, for example), and sweet.

The oriental family is usually subdivided into two, the amber (principally the resins) and the spicy (ginger, clove, etc.). Some perfume houses place an additional subfamily between the florals and the orientals, called the semi-orientals.[2] It is based on the spices, resins and sweeter elements of the oriental family, with lavender, rose or other florals added.

*Chypre* fragrances are mostly fruity (the citruses), but can also include some florals (possibly the less obviously flowery fragrances such as chamomile).

The overlap between *chypre* and *fougère* seems to be the location of the woody subfamily, generally speaking, although again, different perfume houses have slightly different classifications. The heavier fragrances, such as patchouli, are most often placed here.

*Fougère* fragrances include fresh (grassy scents), green (the herbs), and fresh-floral, for example, clover. This last subfamily overlaps with the floral family.

Male fragrances are divided slightly differently – and rather more simply than those for women. The floral group is disregarded, in the main, although certain flower oils (rose, for example) are still used to add a particular quality to the perfume. The main categories are *chypre*, oriental and *fougère*.

The *chypre* group for men includes the woods (pine, cedar), citrus and leather. The leather subfamily includes the heavier, smoky scents of leather, tobacco and birch tar, and is an extraordinarily masculine group.

The orientals include amber and spicy as for female fragrances, but tend to concentrate on the less sweet elements – less vanilla, more frankincense.

The *fougère* family includes lavender as a subfamily all to itself; appropriate given the much-loved place the fragrance has had throughout the millennia. Other subdivisions are fresh (the herbs) and wood-amber (the warmer, more exotic woods – cypress and sandalwood, for example.)

Having picked my way through that minefield – and in the hope I haven't made any critical errors! – I will turn to the perfumes themselves ...

It is clear from the foregoing that there are an amazing variety of 'ingredients' available for the professional perfumer to experiment with. A large number of the natural fragrances now have synthetic counterparts – not surprisingly, since, given the vagaries of the weather and other natural phenomena, using synthetic ingredients may be the only way to maintain a consistent and acceptable product year after year – and the modern-day perfumer needs to be as much a chemist as a trained and practised artist.

Perfumes have three to five main parts, known as 'notes'. Generally speaking, these are called the top, middle and base notes, and where each element is placed depends on how quickly they evaporate when exposed to air (how volatile they are). Top notes evaporate most quickly, then middle notes, and finally the base notes. Interestingly, there seems to be a link between the volatility of an essential oil and its effect on the human body – in aromatherapy, at any rate. Top notes uplift and invigorate, middle notes balance the physical systems of the body, while base notes are calming. The top notes of a fragrance determine how the perfume smells when it is first applied, the middle notes give the fragrance its distinctive character, while the base notes provide its staying power and depth of feeling.

Top notes include the light citrus oils – lemon, grapefruit, orange – eucalyptus, basil, bergamot, chamomile, lavender, neroli and juniper berry.

Middle notes include such fragrances as marjoram, clary sage, pine, rose, rosewood, ylang-ylang, geranium, lemongrass and violet.

Base notes include cedarwood, sandalwood, vanilla, vetivert, myrrh, frankincense, cinnamon, oakmoss, rosemary and patchouli.

The way in which the perfume develops on the skin, from the first sharp scent of the top notes through to the warm, deep fragrance of its base notes, is called the 'journey through time' by Guerlain.

The perfume house of Guerlain (possibly the oldest in the world: it has been in existence for 175 years at the time of writing and has been a family business all that time) creates its fragrances using a five-fold process: top notes (usually citrus), head notes (herbs), the heart note (usually floral), base notes (woods, spice and moss), and the deep base notes (usually oriental). It was the first perfume house to use synthetic material in a perfume – Jicky, a fragrance for both men and women, unveiled in 1889.

The process of creating a new fragrance starts, as do most things, with an idea, based in this case on what sort of person the fragrance should appeal to. The experienced perfumer will choose the appropriate elements to suggest the mood, feeling or attitude he intends; then the long and involved process of blending the essential oils (and other ingredients) to create the fragrance begins. Once the desired fragrance is achieved, the perfume is left to age, a little like wine, for up to a year. The name and the packaging then complete the process, and a new fragrance is born.

Perfumes come in different strengths, depending on the ratio of the essential oil to the alcohol that acts as a preservative and the water that dilutes the fragrance to the desired concentration. Perfume, the most intense and most expensive form, contains between 15 and 30% of the essential oil, the remaining 70 to 85% of the volume being comprised of 90 to 95% alcohol and 5 to 10% water. *Eau de parfum* uses less oil – 8 to 15% – and less alcohol – 80 to 90%, while *eau de toilette* uses 4 to 8% oil. *Eau de cologne* uses only 3 to 5% oil to 70% alcohol.

## Fixatives

Perfumes need a fixative of some sort to give them staying power, preventing their speedy evaporation and prolonging their life. Resins (especially gum benzoin), mosses and synthetic substances are all used. In the past, animal substances (which, it must be confessed, are the most effective fixatives) were also employed – musk, civet, castor and ambergris – all of them requiring the abuse, and often the death, of the animal from which they are obtained. There are now synthetic replacements for these natural substances.

### Musk
Natural musk is probably the most expensive natural product in the world – weight for weight it costs five times as much as gold. Musk is secreted from the abdominal gland of the male musk deer,

and demand for the product has led to a decline of 50% in the Russian musk deer population in the last ten years – with predictions that the species will be on the very brink of extinction within the next ten. There has been a perfectly adequate 'nature identical' substance available for quite some time, making it quite unnecessary to use genuine musk in the perfume and cosmetics industry, although this would probably not be suitable for the substance's other main use, as an ingredient in Chinese medicine – which is somewhat worrying, given the Chinese record regarding other animals used in native medicine (most notably the tiger, now also facing extinction).

### Civet
The civet is a weasel-like animal native to Africa and Asia. There are around 17 species of the creature, living in varied habitats – plain, forest and brush. The civet (which comes from a gland under the tail) which is used as a perfume fixative is used by the animal to mark its territory, much as an unneutered cat will spray to identify its home ground.

### Castor
Castor is produced by beavers. Both male and female animals have scent glands at the rear of their bodies which secrete castoreum, the basis for the fixative. Castoreum was also a popular medicine in the Middle Ages – beavers ate willow bark, and the salicylic acid (the basic constituent of aspirin) contained in the bark acted as an analgesic.

### Ambergris
Ambergris – grey amber – is an oily substance found in the intestines of sperm whales, those magnificent but now sadly depleted monarchs of the sea.

### A Note about Choosing Perfumes
Whether you are choosing a commercially produced fragrance or making up one of your own, it is important not to try too many on your skin at any one time. One perfume on each wrist is quite sufficient, otherwise your sense of smell can become confused – and in any case, putting different perfumes too close to each other tends to

make the fragrances blend into each other until it's impossible to distinguish between them.

*Always* wear a perfume for at least a couple of hours, sniffing frequently to see how it wears on your skin, before deciding whether it is for you. Everyone's skin is slightly different and reacts differently to the elements in a perfume – that's half the pleasure of experimenting with fragrances, trying out different ones until you find the one that's right for you.

## Making Your Own

It is extremely easy to make your own perfume at home. All you need are some essential oils, vodka and bottled distilled water (which you should be able to buy from the chemist). Oh, and a notebook to record every step of your recipe: there are few things more frustrating than to create a perfume that smells absolutely wonderful, and which you feel is a perfect, fragrant statement of your personality and temperament, only to find you cannot remember the exact ingredients. Of course, in trying to recreate the original aroma you might end up finding one that smells even better, but it is not guaranteed, so taking the time necessary to note down the quantities is well worth the effort. After all, the fragrance you create will be absolutely unique to you. If, as often happens, it becomes a personal trademark, you will certainly want to be able to make more.

Vodka is the best preservative for perfume making at home: its own aroma is minimal and does not usually spoil the fragrance you are creating. Bottled spring water can be employed if distilled water is unavailable. It is important that the bottles in which you make, and into which you decant, your perfume are sterilised. (The sterilising tablets used for babies' bottles are perfectly adequate.) Once you have created your fragrance, leave in a dark place for at least six weeks for the perfume to age before bottling.

It is quite possible to make perfume items without using essential oils, although the fragrances will not be as intense or long lasting. However, there can be a lot of pleasure to be had out of the process. Below are some fairly easy recipes you might like to try.

## Bramble Leaf and Elderflower Aftershaves

The ingredients for these two simple aftershave recipes can be gathered on a country walk – elderflowers in the spring, and bramble leaf in the autumn. Both plants have a cooling, tonic effect on the skin. The procedure for making the aftershave is the same for both. Simply simmer about a pint/half a litre of the plant material in water for half an hour to release the fragrance, then cool and strain. Add more water if the aroma is too intense (but remember it will gradually fade once applied), and pour into scrupulously clean bottles. Add a tablespoonful of vodka or other white, relatively fragrance-free spirit as a preservative if you so wish. Otherwise, only make up small amounts of the aftershave, and keep (well-labelled!) in the fridge.

## Rosewater and Lavender Water

Gather the rose petals (any kind will do for the initial stage) two to three hours after sunrise, on a fine day. Crush the petals (a kitchen mortar and pestle are ideal, though if you have a lot of petals it can be a little time-consuming) and leave them to soak, covered, in their own liquid for six hours. Strain through a cloth, squeezing to extract all the liquid. Pour the liquid over fresh, whole petals, the more fragrant the better. This 18th-century recipe calls for 1lb/500g of petals to each pint/half litre of rose water, but adjust the quantities accordingly, cover and leave to stand for twenty-four hours.

To distil the rosewater, either use a still, or improvise with a large saucepan, a heavy bowl and some muslin or cheesecloth. Pour the rose-petal-rosewater mixture into the pan, stand the bowl in the centre, and cover the top of the pan with the fabric. Cover tightly and simmer gently: the steam will condense onto the pan lid, drop onto the cloth and drip into the bowl. (You need to check every now and then to ensure the pan does not boil dry.) Allow it to cool in the bowl, then decant into sterilised bottles. The rosewater can be used as a cosmetic – it is a soothing tonic for the skin – or as a flavouring in food.

Lavender water is made in the same way, according to the 18th-century recipe. For a fragrant change, try steeping the lavender flowers in rosewater for a few days before distilling.

## Lip Salve

An adaptation of an 18th-century lip salve – over a low heat, melt together 1oz/28g of myrrh resin, 2oz/56g of beeswax, 4oz/112g of honey, and 6oz/170g of home-made rose oil – or substitute two to three drops of rose essential oil. (This makes quite a substantial amount of the salve – try potting some up for a friend.) Pour into small pots and leave to cool, then use sparingly. This is not only gloriously fragrant, but glossy and wonderfully soothing for dry, chapped or generally neglected lips …

# 9
# *Crafty Perfumes!*

Making your own perfumed items at home is a good way of developing your sense of smell, as well as learning about the effects of different fragranced materials. It is also an ideal stress-reducing exercise, a great way to perfume your home without using chemical sprays, and a lot of fun.

A brief note before you start – try to write down the ingredients and the quantities you use in any of the following suggestions. A record of the 'recipes' will be invaluable when you find one you particularly like and want to recreate at a later date.

## *Pot pourri*

The name comes from 18th century French and means, literally, 'rotten pot' (i.e. decaying matter in a jar), but do not let that put you off! The delicate fragrance of *pot pourri* in a room is a positive delight. There are an enormous variety of *pot pourri* mixes commercially available, from craft shops, specialist shops, or even supermarkets, but it is far more satisfying to make your own.

The ideal *pot pourri* should look attractive as well as smelling pleasant. It is useful to decide what effect you desire before starting – a clean, fresh welcoming scent for the entrance hall, for example, or a rich, sensual fragrance for the bedroom. Keep an eye out for interesting and attractive bowls, and try to match them to your chosen purpose. A solid clay container, for example, could be ideal for a cottage garden mix, a sturdy wooden box for a woodland blend, a large, nacreous shell for the bathroom or a room with a marine theme, or a beautiful glass bowl for a special room. Chinese soup bowls make excellent containers for spicy blends, people trying to give up smoking should use their ashtrays (a great way to remind yourself not to give in), while an old, large brandy glass can bring a nostalgic (or kitsch!) touch to the room. It is even possible to use children's toys – dumper trucks, seaside buckets – for fun.

**Preparations**
The only item that is common to all *pots pourris* is some sort of fixative. There are several different types, but they all have the same effect – they absorb the oils that provide the perfume for the mix, and prolong its life. Ground orris root (the fragrant rhizome of, usually, the iris *Florentina*) is the most commonly recommended, and most effective, fixative, but it can be difficult to find.[1]

However, there are a number of others, amongst them gum benzoin (said to be the equal to orris root powder in effectiveness), cinnamon quills or powder, nutmeg, cloves, oakmoss (*Evernia purpuracea*), angelica and sweet cicely seeds, and vanilla pods. Cinnamon, nutmeg or clove powder would perhaps be the easiest to obtain. (Raid the kitchen spice rack!) To start with, try using about one tablespoonful of mixed fixative and spices to two cups of dried ingredients when making up your mix: as you experiment, you may find you need more or less than this amount. If you find a supplier for orris root powder and intend experimenting with a variety of *pots pourri*s – and remember they can make attractive and thoughtful gifts – it might be worth buying a good supply. Otherwise, as in your choice of container, you are really only limited by your imagination. Leaves, flowers, roots, woods, cones, spices, fruits, berries, seaweed, salt, even alcohol can form the constituents of a *pot pourri* – along with your essential oils, of course. There are two methods of preparing plants for a *pot pourri*, dry and moist. Of the two, the moist method is more time consuming, but results in a more intense, longer lasting fragrance.

The term 'moist' *pot pourri* is something of a misnomer as the mix itself is completely dry. It is the basic method of preparing the main ingredient that involves moisture (brandy, in fact). Into an airtight jar, place a one cm/½ inch layer of strongly fragranced, partially dried petals (rose is the most usual choice) and add a layer of coarse salt, approximately three mm thick. Add a second layer of petals and salt, then sprinkle with a pinch of brown sugar and a few drops of brandy, and press down firmly. Repeat this process, adding sugar and brandy every second layer of salt until the jar is full. Seal the jar and allow the mix to cure for two months. Drain if necessary, then crumble some of the resultant 'cake' of cured petals into a bowl with the other ingredients (spices, fixative, essential oils) to be used for the fragrance required. Try experimenting with small amounts until you find one you particularly like. Mix and leave to blend and dry for another three weeks or so. Moist *pot pourri* is visually unappetising: add it to a small muslin or net bag and disguise it with the flowers, leaves or other materials you desire, or by keeping it in a covered pot, and only opening the lid when you want the fragrance to fill the room.[2]

Drying plants for use in *pot pourri* is quite simple. Sprays of plant material – lavender, rosemary, meadowsweet – large single flowers, and bunches of herbs can be left hanging somewhere warm and dark, upside down in loose bunches, until they have completely dried out. It is easy, if a little time-consuming, to strip the leaves from the sprigs of lavender and rosemary. (It is also advisable to wear light gloves as both leaves and branches can be quite rough.) Petals, buds, woodchips and cones are better laid in single layers on trays and left to dry, again somewhere warm and dark. Soft and fleshy leaves, from herbs, for example, can be dried in the same way, but be prepared for them to shrivel and become very brittle. If you wish to keep the shape, try drying them between sheets of kitchen towel, but do not press them together too hard or the fragrance will end up on the paper rather than in the leaf! Pick the plants when they are dry – flowers should be collected in bud or just after opening – as they retain their colour, scent and shape better than if fully opened. Leave all plant materials to dry thoroughly before use, and make sure the materials are not too tightly bunched together to avoid the risk of rotting. Drying can take from days for leaves, to weeks for rosebuds.

Once the plant materials have dried, it is time to mix your ingredients together, along with the essential oil(s) you have chosen to create the effect you want. Then place them in an airtight container for four to six weeks, shaking the container gently every day for the first week and thereafter checking every now and then to see how the fragrance is developing. Once it has reached the intensity you desire, it is ready for use. Place in your chosen bowl and enjoy!

The fragrance is subtle, and may not be tremendously long lasting – you are using natural ingredients here, not chemicals. When the aroma begins to fade, add a few drops of the essential oil blend and gently mix. A wooden spoon is ideal for this.

**Floral**

If you have your own garden, try harvesting some of the leaves and petals of your plants: rose (either the petals or whole dried rosebuds), lavender and rosemary are the traditional plants, but many more can be used, such as violet, carnation, pinks, honeysuckle, elderflower, wallflower, freesia. Most flowers with a scent will retain their fragrance, albeit generally in a more delicate, less intense form, after drying. Try also drying some flowers for their colour and shape rather than their scent – hydrangea, marigold, nasturtium, daisy, cornflower, fuchsia and sea lavender (*Statice*) are all worth trying.

If you are in a hurry, don't have the room, or simply cannot be bothered to wait for everything to dry, there are plenty of outlets selling dried flowers, usually in a variety of colours (both natural and artificially coloured). While these will not, in the main, be scented, there is nothing wrong with using them: indeed, sometimes you can achieve the effect you want more easily when someone else has done the time-consuming work! It could also be argued that your choice of perfume is wider if you do not have to restrict yourself to oils that enhance the natural fragrance of the flowers you use – try experimenting to achieve striking and memorable olfactory effects. You can even spray some of the sturdier flowers with silver, metallic or glittering paints to create a boldly dramatic splash of colour – hydrangea flowers are particularly good in this respect. Bear in mind, however, that all dried flowers are brittle and delicate to some degree, and handle them gently.

Experiment with different floral essential oils to find a favourite blend; rose, neroli, lavender, or ylang-ylang are ideal. For dramatic visual effect, try adding some dried globe thistle (*Echinops*), teasel heads, or different varieties of sea holly (*Eryngium*).

### Leafy

Practically all culinary herbs (for example, peppermint, lemon balm, thyme, fennel), 'medicinal' herbs such as hyssop or yarrow, the leaves of scented geraniums, eucalyptus, bay, and sprigs of pine or other conifers (juniper for example) are good candidates for *pot pourri*. Dry them as noted above, and experiment with aromas until you find one you like. Bear in mind that some herbs are stronger then others – sage in particular can be overpowering if you use too much. Add the herbal essential oils – basil, rosemary or peppermint, for example – to enhance the blend.

### Woody

Pine cones, wood shavings (cedar and sandalwood if you are lucky enough to find a supplier. If not, even woodchips from common woodland trees add a rich undertone to the blend), acorns, sycamore or linden seedpods all come into this category. Some will add visual texture rather than any obvious fragrance, but even if the scent is almost undetectable, it will nevertheless add depth to your mix. Cedarwood, sandalwood, cypress and pine are good oils to try with a woody blend.

### Spiced

Cinnamon sticks (whole or crushed), whole cloves, whole star anise, halved or chopped nutmeg are all excellent in a spicy blend. To add depth, mix orris root powder or gum benzoin with small amounts of crushed spices as well – allspice, cloves, mace, cinnamon, ginger. Raid your spice rack and see what olfactory delights you can create! Fennel, clove, juniper or ginger essential oils are useful in these *pots pourris*.

### Fruits

For a zesty, fresh element to your *pot pourri*, try mixing in some grated orange or lemon peel. Alternatively, dry quartered orange, lemon, lime, slices of kumquat and grapefruit gently in the oven, or peel thin strips from the skin and add them to the mix.

It is quite possible to dry thin slices of fruits such as banana, apple, peach or pear very slowly in a very low oven (remember the aim is to dry the fruit thoroughly, not cook it). Try very thin slices of kiwi fruit, star fruit or even strawberries for decoration. A little desiccated coconut in a fruity blend adds a slightly exotic touch, wonderful for warm summer days. Lemon, grapefruit and orange are good complementary oils for a fruity mix.

**Seeds**
Try adding dried *Cotoneaster* berries, rose-hips, hawthorn, rowan and elder berries, peppercorns, cassia buds (sweet and musky), dried sloes, cardamom seeds, juniper berries, dried chillies, alder catkins, dried baby sweetcorn, grass heads, hops, ears of wheat and corn, clematis seedheads, even sunflower or watermelon seeds to your *pot pourri*. Not all are fragranced, but they will add texture and visual impact to the blend. I like to use a blend of tea tree and cedarwood oils, with a drop of myrrh or frankincense, in a seed-predominant mix. (It is best to make small amounts of this mix, and use in little bowls. Also be careful that children don't mistake it for a bowl of sweets!) Make sure the seeds you use are non-poisonous, so avoid yew and deadly nightshade berries, for example.

It is quite possible to experiment with other, less obvious *pot pourri* ingredients. Small pieces of assorted types of dried seaweed can form the basis of an interesting mix (though you need to be careful to keep it as dry as possible). Try adding pebbles, coarse sea salt, dried sea holly (*Eryngium*) and shells. There are no obvious essential oils that smell of the sea shore, but try experimenting with myrrh, tea tree and juniper berry to create a fresh, unusual fragrance. In a glass bowl on a sunny windowsill, such a *pot pourri* can become quite a focal point for a hallway or lounge.

**A Note about Wild Plants**
Many native wild plants have a wonderful fragrance and very attractive appearance. When out and about, try smelling the flowers, and brushing or gently squeezing the leaves of the plants around you – you may well be surprised at the fragrances you find. Some of these will be ideal for inclusion in your own *pot pourri*, but before picking anything, please make sure you observe a few simple 'rules'.

Firstly, some native plants are extremely rare and protected by law. To be on the safe side, try to have at least a nodding acquaintance with them (countryside and conservation organisations will be able to provide more information). Use common sense, as well: one small plant growing by itself in a woodland glade is quite likely to be a member of a rare species, while acres of flowering, fragrant gorse on a hillside is anything but!

Only pick what you need. Never dig up a wild plant, and be very sparing when collecting from a small population of your chosen plant. Always leave plenty of leaves, flowers and/or seedheads. Best of all, from an environmentally sensitive point of view, take just a little seed and grow the plants in your own garden.

**Seasonal Suggestions**
In the spring, aim for a light, delicate fragrance. Try hyacinth, lily of the valley, early violets, lilac, apple blossom (a truly wonderful, if ephemeral fragrance) and scented narcissi: use tiny amounts of bergamot, tagetes, lavender and/or chamomile essential oils to enhance and prolong the perfume.

Finding summertime *pot pourri* ingredients is, generally speaking, not a problem! Experiment with the floral essential oils – rose, ylang-ylang, geranium, neroli – or the delightfully green aromas of basil or peppermint.

Autumn is when the spices come into their own – cloves, cinnamon, ginger, star anise – blended with mixed berries, dried fruits and citrus peel, and autumn flowers for colour and texture. Try essential oils of juniper berry and cedarwood, and grapefruit and lemon, with perhaps just a hint of lavender.

Rich warm woods, cones, evergreen leaves and herbs such as rosemary and thyme, daphne and winter heliotrope flowers are perfect for a winter blend. Orange, pine, cypress, rosewood, sandalwood, frankincense and myrrh are also ideal for the cold season.

Special occasions – engagements, weddings, anniversaries – often have flowers as part of the ceremony. Try drying some of the flowers and adding them to a special *pot pourri* as a nostalgic memento of the occasion.

**A Festive Season *Pot Pourri***
In a shallow bowl (red, green, or gold are appropriate colours for the season: alternatively try a well-polished wooden bowl), mix orris-root

powder, pine cones, pine woodchips, small twigs of pine needles, holly or *Cotoneaster* berries, star anise, cloves, orange peel, ivy leaves (dried in advance: if using fresh leaves, place them in the bowl at the end rather than mixing them with the rest of the ingredients), bay leaves, lemon balm and rosemary. Sprinkle a blend of essential oils into the *pot pourri* mix. Try experimenting with orange, pine, cedarwood, frankincense, myrrh, clove, bergamot and juniper until you find a blend that reminds you of the Yuletide spirit! (You could try mixing the oils with a spoonful or two of brandy for an extra special smoky aroma …) To add sparkle, place a few small tree baubles, golden stars or a *Poinsettia* bract (preferably artificial – it will last longer) on the surface of the mix, and tie a golden ribbon around the bowl.

## Traditional Pomanders

The name 'pomander' comes from the thirteenth century *pomum ambrae*, meaning 'apple of amber'. Amber – fossilised conifer tree resin dating back 50 million years or so – was traditionally used for purification and to protect against illness. In ancient times it was burned as an incense to ward off disease and ease the pains of childbirth: in the nineteenth century, its reputation as a purifying agent led to it being carved into the mouthpieces of pipes and cigarette holders. This reputation, and the fact that the aromatic material used in making the spherical pomander would have rendered it a brownred colour, is the most likely explanation for the original name – pomanders were carried to ward off disease.

In Elizabethan times, citrus fruits replaced the doubtless somewhat messy balls of plant material used for the original pomanders: oranges were compact, kept their shape, smelt delicious in themselves and were sturdy enough to be studded with the cloves that not only helped keep illnesses at bay but also sweetened the air around the carrier's person. The wealthy carried larger versions of the pomander in 'pouncets' (decorative boxes): these were the ancestors of the aromatic china globes that used to be popular for hanging in wardrobes to keep away moths and fragrance clothes.

Pomanders are easy to make, and in doing so you have the satisfaction of keeping alive an ancient and fragrant tradition.

Lightly score the skin of a whole, firm orange into quarters with a sharp knife. (You can dribble a few drops of orange essential oil into the grooves, to enhance the fragrance, if you so choose.) Pin fabric tape around the orange to mark where the decorative ribbon will later be tied. Avoiding the taped areas, stud the orange all over with cloves, first making holes with a large needle to avoid ending up with a pile of cloves with broken stems! With a little practice and forward planning, it is possible to form the cloves into different shapes and designs on the orange skin.

Remove the tape from the orange. Mix together a small amount of orris root and/or cinnamon powder, bergamot, orange or lemon essential oils in a plastic bag, add the clove-studded orange and shake gently until the fruit is liberally coated with the powder. Remove the pomander from the bag, shake to remove any excess powder, then wrap in tissue paper and leave somewhere warm and dry for a couple of weeks. Decorate with ribbons arranged so that they will support the fruit and allow you to hang the orange from a further loop of ribbon at the top.

Hang the finished pomander in the wardrobe, or a small room such as a WC, to repel insects and fragrance the air. When the fragrance starts to fade, place a few drops of orange and/or clove oil on the ribbon or the orange.

Another form of pomander involves making a small bag or pouch and filling it with an adapted *pot pourri* mix. Use rose petals, a little orris-root powder, eight to ten cloves (bruise them slightly first), rosemary and a little lavender. Add just a drop or two or lavender, rosemary or rose essential oil (or pine or cedarwood for a man), sew the bag shut, and place in your underwear drawer. The fragrance will permeate your clothing, and help keep moths and other insects at bay.

## Herb Pillows

Herb pillows are very easy to create, and can make all the difference between a restless night and a sound sleep.

The inner bag should be made of clean, pure cotton, preferably organically grown to avoid any trace of the pesticides usually sprayed onto cotton crops. If this is not possible, wash the material thoroughly in warm water to which you have added a drop or two of tea tree and lavender essential oils. The basic ingredients of a herb pillow are dried lavender (flowers and leaves) and dried hops, which are available cheaply from any shop selling home-brewing equipment and ingredients. It takes a surprisingly large amount of dried lavender to fill even a small pillow, so if drying your own, make sure you cut plenty of branches!

Try drying other useful herbs and flowers to add to the lavender. Rose petals are wonderful for de-stressing and bringing pleasant dreams; lemon balm is calming and soothing; chamomile relieves anxiety and fretfulness; and scented geranium leaves ease nervousness, especially before tests (try the apple-scented variety if you can find it). Enjoy experimenting. Once you have all your chosen dried ingredients, pour them into the inner bag and shake gently but thoroughly to mix well. Do not overfill – there should be space for the plant material to shift around, especially when shaken. Sew up the open edge of the bag to complete.

The pillow can be used in this form. However, like ordinary bedroom pillows, it will stay cleaner and fresher if you make a cover to protect it (remember, you can't wash a herb pillow!) The cover should be made of a natural material – cotton is best – and can be any colour or pattern, as simple or as elaborately decorated as you wish. (I usually embroider designs on mine.) Use an ordinary pillowcase as a basic pattern, ensuring that the cover fits the pillow quite closely. Your herb pillow will give you years of service: just shake it gently every now and then to release more fragrance.

Herb pillows are not always the most comfortable things to lie on, but leaving one on your pillow during the day, and having it close to you during the night, will ensure that you receive the full benefit of the herbs you have chosen.

## Scented Candles

If you already make your own candles, simply add a few drops of your chosen essential oils or oil blend to the melting wax and mix thoroughly. If you have never tried the art, there are numerous kits and instructions available from craft shops. However, if you feel like trying your hand without going to much expense or effort, try recycling those small candles known as night lights or tea lights.

You will need some fine wick (available from craft shops, usually on a cardboard spool similar to the coarser varieties of sewing thread: buy the fabric type, not the waxed – it is easier to use), wax – either bought as granules, or just stubs and pieces of old candles, a small saucepan (an old milk pan with a pouring lip is ideal), some spent matches and a sturdy sewing needle with a large hole. If you use a fragrancer, you probably already have some empty aluminium 'cases' (if not, and you use the fragrancer a lot, you soon will have!)

Remove the small metal clip at the bottom of the case and, using the needle, 'sew' a short length of wick through the centre (tie a knot or two to stop the wick from pulling through.) Place a spent match across the case and rest the end of the wick against it – it does not matter if the wick seems too long at this point; it can always be trimmed to the right length later. Melt a small amount of wax in the saucepan over a very low heat and carefully add your chosen oil, keeping your face back from the pan. (At such a low temperature the likelihood of the oil igniting is practically non-existent, but it is always best to err on the side of caution.) Agitate the wax to mix in the oil, then pour the scented wax carefully into the night light cases, ensuring that the wick stays above the surface. Leave to set – which only takes about ten to fifteen minutes – use sharp scissors to cut the wick to the right length, and the candles are ready for use.

Ceramic or glass night light holders are available in different designs and shapes – animals, houses, etc. – and are ideal for use with fragranced candles. It is also possible to buy – or paint for yourself – coloured glass, open topped containers designed to hold small candles. These are ideal for use with fragranced night lights – attractive to look at and wonderful to smell – though of course they shouldn't be placed where they can be knocked over. Try using different colours and perfumes for different moods or seasons: scarlet, green and gold coloured glass for Yule, with pine-scented candles; pink and apricot with rose or sandalwood for the guest bedroom; amethyst and emerald with patchouli or ylang-ylang for newly-weds; yellow and orange with grapefruit or juniper berry for the kitchen.

These make charming, loving gifts for friends and family, especially if you use their favourite fragrances and colours, or design them to match or contrast different rooms in the home.

## Incense

It is possible to make, or at the very least to blend, your own incense at home. There are specialist shops selling the basic ingredients – granules of the resins such as myrrh and frankincense, for example, and the shaped charcoal blocks that are the most convenient way of burning incense at home. Place them in an ashtray or heat-proof dish, set alight, and wait until the flame has died down and the surface grey and ashy before adding the incense, otherwise it can spit quite badly. Having hot incense grains land on your skin is a sobering – and scarring – experience ... However, it is quite easy to experiment with your own plant material.

Try chips of fragrant woods – willow smells sweet as it burns. Dry some of the fragrant flowers in the garden and see how they smell when smouldering on the charcoal block. Copy the classical Greeks and Romans and burn some basil, rosemary, thyme or lavender leaves. Do be sure to keep notes of your experiments, so that you can recreate blends you particularly like or avoid ones you do not like. On that subject, it might be wise to perform your experiments out of doors, initially; that way, if you find you loathe the fragrance, you won't have to suffer it in your house!

# 10
# *Haunting Fragrances*

Although not common, there have been cases of fragrances associated with hauntings. In the UK, these are usually found in ancient houses, such as Bramshill, near Hartley Wintney in Hampshire.

The house is very old – it was mentioned twice in the Domesday Book (1086) – and has a number of apparitions, including a grey lady, a green man, an invisible child who takes hold of visitors' hands, and a little old man with a beard. The building is reputed to be the scene of 'The Legend of the Mistletoe Bough', in which a young bride, caught up in a game of hide-and-seek during her wedding day festivities, found herself locked into a chest and died there. A room on the first floor of the house is filled with an entirely inexplicable but intensely sweet smell of lilac.

Brede Place, in East Sussex, dates from the 14th century (although it was added to in later years) and is a beautiful and fascinating old house set in well-kept grounds. The building is an ideal retreat and has been used as a source of inspiration for writers, artists and sculptors – and the odd smuggler and pair of lovers – over the centuries. As well as the ghosts of a murdered woman and a priest, the house is occasionally and unseasonably filled with the perfume of violets. No one knows why, although it may not be unreasonable to assume it may have something to do with the slain woman ...

The smell of incense seems to be a fairly popular ghostly motif in old houses. This is perhaps fairly understandable at St Mary's Church, in London NW10, and Beaulieu Abbey, Hampshire, since incense is most often associated with religious observances. Borley Rectory, Suffolk, also had spells when the scents of incense and violets out of season filled the building – at least, such was the case until it was burned to the ground in 1939. Bayham Abbey (now a ruin) in Kent also manifests the fragrance of burning incense, along with the sweet sound of faint music and chanting in Latin. The fact that the charming Bluebell Inn in

Leicestershire was reputedly built on the site of an old monastery might explain why the building is filled and pervaded by the exotic smell of incense during the night – especially around the time of the full moon. (The place is also haunted by a hunchback, who makes his way to the Inn's old well at night.) It is less clear why the same fragrance should appear in such a place as Gawsworth Hall, in Cheshire.

This lovely, half-timbered 15th-century house is home to the ghosts of a lady, usually seen in the courtyard, and a capering jester in a nearby spinney, but the most interesting phenomenon is the sweet smell of incense that gradually fills one of the bedrooms. The bedroom is immediately below a priest's hole (a secret chamber built into certain houses and used as a hiding place for persecuted Roman Catholic priests during the 16th and 17th centuries): in the 1920s a human skeleton was found near the oratory (a small room devoted to private prayer) that was also part of the house. It is impossible not to speculate that the remains may have been those of a priest sheltered by the family in the distant past, who died there, still firm in his faith. Perhaps, instead of a ghostly apparition, the smell of incense – used in the Catholic Mass – serves as the refined spectre of his dedication.

An unusual – and frequently frustrating! – ghostly smell is that of cooking. The Old Pest House, near Knebworth, Hertfordshire, has been haunted by the smell of frying bacon and eggs for many years, even when the old building has been empty for months. Another intriguing case concerns Chiswick House, London W4. Originally built in the 1730s more as a meeting place for artists and politicians (though not necessarily at the same time), the building became a private lunatic asylum at the beginning of the 19th century, and was then taken over by the Department of the Environment in the 1950s and restored to its former splendour. During the restoration, a strong smell of frying bacon and eggs was noticed – sometimes for a couple of days in a row, sometimes briefly after a break of a few months – even though no cooking ever took place in the building. Interestingly, the smell was only present in the north wing where the kitchen used to be, more than a century ago ...

Leith Hall, in the Grampians in Scotland, is haunted by the smells of cooking food, and also camphor, as well as the ghostly apparitions of a Victorian lady, a child, and a Scotsman with a bandaged head. But perhaps the most bizarre occurrence, however, is in a dental surgery in Regents Park, London NW1, where the smell of frying bacon and roasting coffee occasionally wafts through the building – to the presumed frustration of the patients!

One extremely strange example of an odorous haunting was at the Ambassador Bowling Club in Basildon, Essex. Although a fairly modern building, the ghost of a man in workman's clothes was seen in Lane 17, accompanied by the smells of a farmyard. On investigation, it was found that the club had been built on land where farm buildings had stood at the beginning of the 20th century. There had been a double murder at the farm, and in 1940 a young man had committed suicide.

One of the bedrooms of Elvey Farm in Kent, a 500-year-old farm building converted into a detached house, was often filled with the distinctive smell of burning wool. (The building also appeared to be haunted by the ghost of a young man who opened and unlocked doors and switched lights on.)

Broughton Hall, in Surrey, and the private home of Busheygate, Sussex, were both subject to the strong smell of pipe tobacco, even though no one living there smoked a pipe.

Less savoury smells have also been known to haunt buildings. A London hotel was the scene of a particularly unpleasant occurrence when a guest awoke to the sensation of floating above a pit from which wafted the rank smell of decaying vegetable material and fungus. It was rumoured that the hotel had been built above a plague pit, where the bodies of the dead – and, reputedly, sometimes the living – were dumped during the plagues of the 14th century and onwards.

A manor house in Warwickshire saw the apparition of a nun who, although in an advanced state of bodily decay, rushed up to some visitors and fell to her knees before them, raising her hands in appeal. A nauseating smell of decay and putrefaction came from her rotting body, even though, since she vanished almost immediately, she was obviously incorporeal. There was no physical matter to provide the stench.

As a final note, be wary should you ever need to summon Astaroth, the twenty-ninth spirit in the second hierarchy of the 72 chief spirits of the *Goetia* – the *Book of Evil Spirits*. His breath is so 'noisome' he can use it as an extremely dangerous weapon.

## Saintly Perfumes

As well as fragrances associated with ghosts and demons, there are perfumes linked with saints – usually the scent of roses which often issues from their opened tombs instead of the scent of decay.

The patroness of sailors, Saint Rosalia of Palermo, in Sicily, lived during the 12th century. At the age of sixteen, she dedicated herself to God, withdrawing to live in a cave near the summit of Mount Pellegrino. She later died there alone, but when her body was discovered some time later, it had not decayed, and her head was adorned with a crown of incorruptible roses – from Paradise, or so the legend goes.

Saint Rose, born in 1586 in Peru, was the daughter of a Spanish family impoverished by unwise speculation. A beautiful woman, she took vows of chastity early in her life, and reputedly ruined her face with a lotion made of pepper and quicklime to discourage her many suitors. She worked in the garden during the day, and sewed through the nights in order to support her parents, and by choice lived a life of penance and deprivation, which contributed to the illness that led to her death at the age of 31.

When, in 1671, Pope Clement X was requested to canonise the young woman, he refused, saying a saint from the New World was as likely as a rain of roses – at which a shower of roses is said to have fallen from the sky, persuading the Pope to change his mind ...

The patron saint of perfume makers is Mary Magdalen.

## The Rosary

The rosary probably originated in the East, and the method of manufacture has remained much the same for millennia. Rose petals are dried, then crushed to a powder, mixed with rose water, carefully shaped into pellets and strung onto a cord. The strings of rose beads are thoroughly dried, then polished.

The beads are run gently through the fingers as an aid to meditation or prayer. The rosary used by Chinese and Japanese Buddhists is strung with 108 beads, each one represents a prayer for forgiveness for each of the 108 sins known to the human race. Other Buddhists use a rosary of 99 beads, the Greek rosary has 100, and the Russian Orthodox 103. The rosary used by the Catholic Church has 165 beads in fifteen sets of ten small beads and fifteen large.

Each small bead is known as an Ave Maria (Hail Mary), while the large are known as Pater Noster (Our Father). The beads are handled and counted as a set number of the prayers are recited.

Counting the beads was originally a way for the early Christians, who were mostly illiterate, to memorise prayers. Nowadays, the soothing, repetitive motions of handling the beads is an aid to concentration, enabling the mind to focus on meditation or prayer.

## Astrological Fragrances

Over the millennia, the twelve archetypes of the signs of the zodiac and their ruling planets have accrued a wealth of correspondences (objects, elements and associations specific to each individual sign) – it is natural that fragrance should be amongst them.

One of the earliest records of the fragrances associated with both the planets and the signs of the zodiac comes from Cornelius Agrippa. Born on 14 September 1486, Henry Cornelius Agrippa spent most of his life in the study of the occult, and in 1533 he published three books, known collectively as 'Occult Philosophy'. The first volume – *The Philosophy of Natural Magic* – contains the details of how to create the appropriate 'fumes' for each planet (only seven were recognised at the time). These could then be used, often as incense, in rituals concerning each of the planets. For example, to inspire love in another a rite to Venus could be performed, or for success in a business venture, a dedication to Jupiter. Some of the ingredients are obscure, while others are a little on the gory side!

**The Sun**: blend saffron, ambergris, musk, lignum aloes, lignum balsam, the fruit of the laurel, cloves, myrrh and frankincense with the brain of an eagle or the blood of a white cock.

The Sun governs the resins, frankincense, mastic, gum benzoin, storax, labdanum, ambergris and musk.

**The Moon**: crush together the head of a dried frog, the eyes of a bull, the seed of white poppy, frankincense and camphor, and mix with the blood of a goose.

The Moon governs the leaves of all plants, but especially the myrtle and bay tree.

**Saturn**: mix black poppy seed, henbane, mandrake root, crushed lodestone (magnetite), myrrh, the brain of a cat and the blood of a bat.

Saturn governs aromatic roots such as pepperwort.

**Jupiter**: mix together ash seed, lignum aloes, storax (a vanilla-scented resin from the sub-tropical or tropical *Styrax* tree or shrub), gum benzoin, crushed lapis lazuli, the ends of peacock feathers, the blood of a stork or swallow, or the chopped brain of a hart.

Jupiter governs odoriferous fruits such as nutmeg and cloves.

**Mars**: blend euphorbium, bedellium, gum ammoniac, hellebore root, crushed lodestone, a little sulphur, the brain of a hart, the blood of a man and the blood of a black cat.

Mars governs fragrant woods – cypress, sanders (sandalwood?), lignum aloes and lignum balsam.

**Venus**: mix musk, ambergris, lignum aloes, red roses, crushed red coral, the brain of sparrows and the blood of pigeons.

Venus governs sweet flowers such as roses and violets.

**Mercury**: blend mastic (the resin of the Mediterranean *Pistacia lentiscus* tree), frankincense, cloves, *cinque-foil*, achate stone, the brain of a fox or weasel and the blood of a magpie.

Mercury governs the peels of fragrant woods and fruit – cinnamon, mace, lemon – and aromatic seeds such as cardamom and fenugreek.

The fragrances allocated to the zodiac signs are: Aries – myrrh; Taurus – pepperwort (*Lepidium campestre*); Gemini – mastic; Cancer – camphor; Leo – frankincense; Virgo – sanders; Libra – galbanum (bitter aromatic resin from the Asian *Ferula galbaniflua* plant); Scorpio – opoponax; Sagittarius – lignum aloes; Capricorn – gum benzoin; Aquarius – euphorbium; Pisces – red storax.

These days the correspondences between the zodiac signs and the most appropriate perfumes is much less strict, depending more on the character of the fragrance rather than its constituents.

Aries fragrances should be bold and dramatic – a perfume or aftershave that makes an unforgettable statement. Fresh citrus aromas are ideal.

Taurus perfumes should be warm, floral and strongly feminine for the women and warm, woody and conservatively masculine for the men. Quality is important to Taurus, and since quality is often measured by how much something costs, the more expensive cosmetics are usually favoured.

Versatile, changeable Gemini is most likely to have a shelf-full of different perfumes and choose them according to the mood of the hour!

Subtle, more traditional fragrances are most appropriate for Cancer – even simple lavender water makes a delicate, understated assertion about Cancer's nostalgic respect for traditional values. All perfumes should be applied with a light hand.

Leo wears rich, spicy fragrances best – but should beware of using too much, as many Leos tend to think that more is better,

Virgo should choose light, herb-scented fragrances, subtle but complex – the sort of aroma that demands a second sniff.

Sophisticated modern fragrances suit Libra best. Librans enjoy luxury and like being pampered, so the more expensive the perfume the better!

Scorpios need deep, dark, musky fragrances to accentuate their innate exotic sensuality.

The fresh, sporty perfumes are ideal for Sagittarius. Pine or light woody fragrances are ideal for the male Sagittarius, while light, breezy perfumes suit the women.

Capricorn respects conservative values and good quality. Favourite fragrances tend to the woody, and are clean, uncomplicated and often quite old – Capricorns tend not to enjoy change, so once a fragrance has been chosen it will probably remain a favourite for life.

Aquarius is the innovator of the zodiac, and will usually be the first to try a new fragrance. Ultra-modern, cool, often synthetic perfumes suit Aquarius well.

The ideal fragrance for Pisces can be either innocently floral or distantly exotic, but should always be delicate, reminiscent of a whisper of perfume on the breeze.

**Fragrant Dreams**
Dreaming of fragrances, and actually being able to smell them, is perhaps less common than the use of the other senses in dreams, but it does occur, and of course, over the years specific meanings have been devised for dream-aromas – much as they have for everything else you might find in a dream. The following are some traditional meanings. As with all dreams, however, your own interpretation of the scents and associated images is far more valid than any list created by another.

**Smells in general**: if the aroma is pleasant, it heralds pleasant times and happy circumstances ahead. If unpleasant, it presages difficulties in relation to how unpleasant you found the odour in the first place: the nastier the smell, the worse the problem.

**Camphor** – a smell of mothballs – traditionally warns against indulging in casual or promiscuous sex: scandal or illness could result.

**Cedar**: A dream featuring the fragrance or the use of cedarwood is an omen of contentment, of finding pleasure with your life, no matter how restricted or humble.

**Herbs**: Any herbal fragrance predicts new and exciting adventures, possibly abroad.

**Incense**: In a dream this presages a lessening of your present worries – unless you did not like the smell, in which case your troubles will become more burdensome!

**Lavender**: In a dream this indicates a pleasant – but not heart-stoppingly exciting – love affair.

**Lilac**: To dream of lilac foretells a broken friendship. This will cause grief at the time, but will later turn out to be a blessing in disguise, as greater grief would have accrued had the relationship continued.

**Lily**: If the lilies were Madonna or calla lilies – large, white and imposing – they herald an increase in status, perhaps a promotion at work and its attendant benefits. However, dreaming of lily-of-the-valley is an omen of domestic happiness and happiness in affairs of the heart.

**Lotus**: Being able to smell the fragrance of lotus in a dream signifies that you will be ecstatically happy in love and romance.

**Mint**: This signifies happiness if you are healthy and an improvement in health if you (or the individual in your dream) is ill.

**Musk**: To smell musk in a dream presages a passionate new love affair.

**Myrtle**: The perfume – and indeed the bush itself – presages popularity, stamina and sexual vigour!

**Paprika**: The sight or smell of this spice in a dream advises you to learn a little self-control, or you risk your health.

**Parsley**: In a dream this heralds success. If growing, you will be successful through your own hard work. If you ate it, the intelligent use of lucky breaks and sudden opportunities will achieve your goal.

**Perfume**: For a woman to dream of using perfume heralds an unusual new affair: for a man to dream of using a fragrance foretells misunderstandings in both personal and business matters. Rich or heady perfume foretells a passionate affair. Lighter, less intense perfumes suggest a pleasant but not exciting affair.

**Roses**: As might be expected, roses in a dream are intimately connected with affairs of the heart. Picking roses heralds great joy. Giving roses to another signifies that you will be wholeheartedly loved. Receiving roses presages unusual social success. Artificial roses, however, mean deceit or jealousy on the part of a trusted friend and are a warning to be careful what you reveal.

# *Table of Essential Oils*

| Oil | Use | Method |
| --- | --- | --- |
| Basil | Colds, fevers, bronchial complaints. Improves circulation | Can be a depressant – use sparingly |
| Bergamot | Sore throats, fevers, mouth infections, problem skin | Bath, vaporiser, massage (Can irritate sensitive skin – use sparingly. Do not use in the sun.) |
| Cedarwood | Eczema, acne, dandruff, alopecia, low sex drive | Skin and scalp rub (in carrier oil), massage, vaporiser |
| Chamomile | Dry/sensitive skin, cramp, muscle aches, rheumatism, emotional stress, stomach complaints | Bath, massage, vaporiser, skin preparations |
| Cypress | Varicose veins, circulatory problems, excessive sweating | Bath, vaporiser, massage. (Avoid if suffering from high blood pressure.) |
| Eucalyptus | Coughs, colds, sinus problems, mental drowsiness | Steam inhalation, vaporiser |

## TABLE OF ESSENTIAL OILS

| | | |
|---|---|---|
| Fennel | Diarrhoea, indigestion, nausea, flatulence, obesity | Bath, massage. Add one drop to a litre of water and drink throughout the day to ease stomach problems |
| Frankincense | Stimulates the immune system, skin regeneration, lifts depression | Massage, vaporiser |
| Geranium | Skin inflammation, over-production of sebum, acne. Eases PMS and menopausal problems | Massage, skin preparations, vaporiser |
| Grapefruit | Combats cellulite, invigorates and disinfects | Bath, vaporiser, sprayed around the house using a plant mister. (Do not use in the sun.) |
| Juniper | High blood pressure, water retention, greasy skin and hair, cellulite | Bath, massage, vaporiser. (Can overstimulate the kidneys – use sparingly.) |
| Lavender | Burns, scalds, cuts, grazes, headaches, migraines, colds, sinus complaints, insomnia | Bath, massage, vaporiser, neat on skin |
| Lemon | High blood pressure, sebum overproduction, colds, boils, warts; as an insect repellent | Bath, massage, vaporiser, sprayed around the house from a plant mister. (Do not use in the sun.) |

## TABLE OF ESSENTIAL OILS

| | | |
|---|---|---|
| Lemongrass | Headaches, sore throat, bronchitis, oily skin, athlete's foot. Insect repellant: deodorant | Massage, vaporiser, one or two drops in trainers or other footware as a deodorant |
| Myrrh | Bronchitis, colds, flu, candida, athlete's foot and other fungal infections, insomnia, stress | Massage, vaporiser |
| Neroli | Anxiety, panic attacks, shock, hysteria, shyness, broken veins, dry/mature skin | Massage, bath, skin preparations, vaporiser |
| Patchouli | Promoting new skin growth; an aphrodisiac | Bath, massage, perfume, vaporiser |
| Peppermint | Colds, coughs, indigestion, heartburn, irritable bowel syndrome. Insect repellent | Steam inhalation, bath, vaporiser, massage. (Use caution if suffering from epilepsy.) |
| Pine | Respiratory problems, as a disinfectant | Vaporiser, bath, steam inhalation, sprayed around house from a plant mister |
| Rose | Circulatory, menstrual and menopausal problems, mature skin, for all women; aphrodisiac and mood balancing | Bath, massage, vaporiser, perfume, skin preparations |

| | | |
|---|---|---|
| Rosemary | Constipation, circulatory problems, stimulating the liver, general fatigue, mental stimulation, problem hair | Bath, vaporiser, hair rinse, massage. (Use caution if suffering from high blood pressure.) |
| Rosewood | Dry and mature skins | Bath, massage, skin preparations, vaporiser |
| Sandalwood | Sunburn, asthma, nausea, itching; aphrodisiac | Bath, massage, skin preparations, vaporiser, perfume |
| Tea Tree | Mouth ulcers, gum disease, rashes, fungal infections, sunburn, airborne germs and viruses; household disinfectant and insect repellent | Bath, mouthwash (diluted in water), vaporiser, sprayed around the house from a plant mister, in warm water to wash down household surfaces |
| Ylang-Ylang | High blood pressure, obstinate skin complaints, impotence, frigidity, sexual tension, anxiety, depression | Bath, massage, vaporiser, perfume |

# A Cautionary Note

In the main, perfumes and their sources are quite safe and pose no danger to the average person. However, there are just a few simple and sensible precautions we need to take when considering different aspects of the subject.

### Aromatherapy
Essential oils are concentrated. When using them, err on the side of caution. Unless advised otherwise by a trained practitioner, do not use them undiluted on your skin or take them internally, and do keep them out of your eyes! (Should any accidentally get into the eye, immediately dilute with a little vegetable carrier oil and then rinse thoroughly with water.) The only exceptions are lavender and tea tree, which can be safely used undiluted on the skin (though not, of course, in the eyes).

There are a few of the more powerful oils that should, perhaps, be avoided during pregnancy – not because they are dangerous in themselves, but because the body is under enough strain already, and the gentler oils are far more appropriate at this time.

**Gentle Oils** (considered safer to use during pregnancy): chamomile roman, geranium, grapefruit, jasmine, lavender, melissa, myrrh, rose.

**Powerful Oils** (better avoided during pregnancy: many of these aren't readily available in any case): aniseed, bergamot, camphor, fennel, hyssop, juniper, nutmeg, parsley seed, pennyroyal, sage, tagetes.[1]

The citrus family of essential oils (sweet and bitter orange, lemon, mandarin, bergamot, lime, grapefruit etc.) can cause burning of the skin in sunlight or other sources of ultra-violet radiation, so avoid using them for at least four hours before sunbathing, and avoid them altogether if going on holiday anywhere sunny.

## Herbalism/Flowers for Food

Common garden herbs have been used for food for millennia, and, as we've seen,[2] a number of well-known garden flowers are also safe and tasty to eat. However, there are some which are toxic to a greater or lesser degree. Please avoid the following (and note that this list is not exhaustive!):

> aconite (monkshood), anemone, buttercup, cedar, celandine, columbine, cyclamen, daffodil, datura (thorn apple), delphinium, euphorbias (spurge), foxglove, fritillaria, all of the hellebores, henbane, horse chestnut, iris, laburnum, lily of the valley, lupin, the nightshades (woody and deadly), Pasque flower, periwinkle, poppy, tobacco (*Nicotiana*), Virginia creeper, yew.

# Notes

**Introduction**

1 Unless you are one of those – fortunately rare – unlucky people with anosmia (an impaired, or absent, sense of smell).
2 Only in general terms, however: there are exceptions.
3 Try smelling them each individually first, and seeing which you prefer. And there are some which may not be safe to use if you are pregnant – please see 'A Cautionary Note' for a list of oils to avoid.

**1. The Sense of Smell**

1 It has been suggested that each receptor cell is sensitive to just one particular kind of molecule, and will not be activated until that molecule actually makes contact.

**2. Perfumes for the Body and the Soul**

1 Indeed, this idea is still used today in rituals to various deities, in pagan lifepaths such as Wicca.
2 The Ebers Papyrus – actually a medical document.
3 The story of how Gilgamesh, king of Uruk in Mesopotamia, attained wisdom, which, almost in passing, provides intriguing insights into the religion, ethics and thoughts on life itself of the time.
4 The great queen, Gilgamesh's mother, who 'knew all knowledge'.
5 The Sun God who was also the god of justice and the driver away of shadows.
6 The reason why the gods decided to destroy the human race is as yet unrevealed. However, one early translation suggests that the Deluge was let loose upon the world of men because the noise they made was so great the gods could not sleep.
7 Known as the Faraway. The only man to whom the gods granted immortality. Gilgamesh wished to question him about life and death.
8 Ishtar – Babylonian goddess of love and war.
9 Psalm 92, v.12.
10 *Nardostachys jatamans* – aromatic plant with reddish purple flowers.
11 *Acorus calamus* – sweet flag, sweet sedge. Highly aromatic reed-like plant.
12 Source: Marco Polo (1254–1324) *The Travels* pp. 58–9.
13 A long-standing motif in religion and mythology – Cerridwen owned the Cauldron of Inspiration, while placing the bodies of the slain in the Cauldron of the Dagda brought them back to life.

**3. Aromatherapy**

1 See 'Herbalism' for more information about this ancient craft.
2 See 'Haunting Fragrances' for more information on astrological correspondences.
3 There is sometimes a regrettable

tendency to regard our distant ancestors as primitive, uncultured beings with no refinement. In the main this is not the case. While visions of Golden Age Utopias are also far from the truth, in a world with fewer people, no pollution, plentiful clean, fresh water and abundant natural resources, the majority lived lives of dignity and self-respect. The work may have been hard, and life sometimes short, but it was by no means as brutal as the popular imagination would have us believe.
4 The Moluccas, in the Malay Archipelago.
5 He also wrote numerous books on the subject of plants for healing, including *The Book of Healing* and *The Canon of Medicine*, which were still in use in France in the middle of the 16th century.
6 There are just a few things to be aware of when using essential oils. See 'A Cautionary Note' for details.
7 Source: *The Fragrant Pharmacy* p.7.
8 There are, alas, always those more than ready to make a fast buck by diluting the oils they sell.
9 For more information about roses, see 'The Fragrant Garden'.
10 And it avoids the health risks associated with synthetic sprays – see 'The Sense of Smell'.
11 Source: *The Fragrant Pharmacy*, p.148.
12 Make up your own by gently heating your chosen flowers – rose petals or lavender, for example – in spring water, then straining and bottling. Add a drop or two of tea tree or lemon oil to keep the flower water clean and clear of bacteria. Shake well after bottling and before use.
13 See 'Crafty Perfumes!' for a few other ideas.

## 4. Herbalism
1 Dr Bach suffered a severe illness in 1917 and, upon his recovery, apparently found he could tell, intuitively, the healing properties of plants, as well as the illnesses – or states of mind – that they could alleviate.
2 The oak has been seen as a symbol of unflinching strength and fortitude since time immemorial.
3 Which, of course, it is, relieving stress and tension, increasing circulation and deep, healthy breathing, and engendering a happier frame of mind – all of which assist recovery from a vast number of ailments. It could be argued that watching a favourite comedy on TV would have the same effect as a glass of diluted zinnia essence – and be a lot cheaper ... (The effect of doing both together is, as far as I am aware, currently unknown, but may well be worth trying.)

## 5. Gardens
1 'God's Garden', Dorothy Frances Gurney.
2 There is growing evidence which suggests that the relatively new science of psychoneuroimmunolgy (which promotes the theory that happy mental states boost our immune systems while stress and unhappiness deplete them) is a valid and beneficial study. See 'The Sense of Smell' for more information.
3 Freely adapted from by the author *The Victorian Language of Flowers*.
4 See Chapter 9 'Crafty Perfumes!' for details of easy projects to try at home using dried flowers and herbs.
5 See Chapters 7 and 9, 'Fragrant Food' and 'Crafty Perfumes!' respectively, for more information.

# NOTES

6. The herbs in the lyrics are parsley, sage, rosemary and thyme.
7. See Chapter 9 'Crafty Perfumes!' for more information.
8. 'Aye' meaning 'ever'.
9. See 'Fragrant Foods' for details of how to make herb vinegars.
10. 'Abortifacient' – causing abortion. The herb is traditionally used for regulating menstruation.
11. A lemniscus is the figure of eight shape that represents infinity. Also known today as a Möbius strip.

## 6. Feng Shui
1. See 'Aromatherapy'
2. See 'Aromatherapy'

## 7. Fragrant Foods
1. In Rome around the time of Nero a small package of spices – cinnamon, pepper, nutmeg and mace – cost more to buy than the trained cook who would be creating extravagant dishes with them.
2. A hot, peppery spice related to cardamom, still used in West African cookery but little-known elsewhere.
3. *Piper longum*, a plant related to the better-known *Piper nigrum* from which today's black pepper is harvested. Long pepper was probably the first pepper variety to be used in the West.
4. Please see 'A Cautionary Note' for a list of flowers that are dangerous to eat, and note that this list is not exhaustive. If you wish to try using a flower not listed in this book, first make sure you find if it is edible or not – your local garden centre or nursery should be able to help you. Alternatively, try contacting one of the countryside associations for information on wildflowers and wild plants.
5. I should add, of course, that as with all alcohol, no matter how alert coffee wine leaves you feeling, you should never try to drive (or operate machinery) after drinking it.

## 8. Perfumes
1. Of course, a cynic would argue that there would not be any personal embarrassment if we had not been pressurised into thinking natural body odours were somehow distasteful by those who make the deodorising products in the first place …
2. Guerlain, for example.

## 9. Crafty Perfumes!
1. You may be able to find a supplier in herb or craft shops in major cities: alternatively, try searching the Internet for a mail order supplier. Use orris+root+powder (or whatever alternative the search engine prefers) as the search string.
2. Source: *The Book of Pot Pourri*, Penny Black, p.98.

## A Cautionary Note
1. Source: *Shirley Price's Aromatherapy Workbook*, Table 4, pp 124–5.
2. Chapter Seven '**Flowers for Food**'.

# *Bibliography*

*The Travels of Marco Polo* Trans. Ronald Latham, Penguin Classics 1958 ISBN 0 14 044057 7

*The Epic of Gilgamesh* Trans. Andrew George, Penguin Press 1999 ISBN 0 713 99196 8

*The Epic of Gilgamesh* Trans. N. K. Sandars, Penguin Classics 1964

*Shirley Price's Aromatherapy Workbook* Shirley Price, Thorsons 1993 ISBN 0 7225 2645 8 (This large book covers the chemistry of essential oils, extraction methods, and plant families in great detail and is essential reading for anyone wishing to explore the science behind aromatherapy.)

*Aromatherapy for Common Ailments* Shirley Price, Gaia Books 1991 ISBN 1 85675 005 1

*The Fragrant Pharmacy* Valerie Ann Worwood, Bantam Books 1999 ISBN 0 553 40397 4

*Essential Aromatherapy* Carole McGilvery & Jimi Reed, Acropolis Books 1993 ISBN 1 873762 26 7

*Mapping the Mind* Rita Carter, Weidenfeld & Nicolson 1998

*Traditional Herbal Remedies* Jenny Plucknett, Parragon 1997 ISBN 0 7525 1724 4

*The Book of Pot Pourri* Penny Black, Dorling Kindersley 1989 ISBN 0 86318 365 4

*Pharaoh's Flowers* F. Nigel Hepper, HMSO 1990 ISBN 0 11 250040 4

*The Rose (Myth, Folklore and Legend)* Ann Mayhew, New English Library 1979 ISBN 450 04448 3

*Ancient Egypt* Ed. David P. Silverman, Duncan Baird Publishers 1997 ISBN 1 900131 80 3

*Wild Flowers of Britain* Roger Philips, Pan Original 1977 ISBN 0 330 25183 X

*The Philosophy of Natural Magic* Henry Cornelius Agrippa

# BIBLIOGRAPHY

*Traditional Herbal Remedies* Jenny Plucknett, Parragon 1997 ISBN 0 7525 1724 4

*The Complete Book of Herbs and Spices* Claire Loewenfeld & Philippa Back, David and Charles 1974 ISBN 0 7153 6251 8

# INDEX

Lemongrass, 43–4,
Lemon Balm, 70
Lilac, 67, 130
Lily of the valley, 67,
Linne, Carl von, 102
Lupin, 65,

Mace, 89
Magnolia, 65,
Marigolds, 92, 99
Marjoram, 70–1, 83
Mary Magdalen, 126
Meadow Sweet, 74
Mint, 18, 45, 71–2, 83, 95, 131
Mouth, 37,
Musk, 25, 106–7
Myrrh, 19, 21, 44, 83

Nasturtium, 92
Nemesia, 65
Neroli, 25, 44, 94
Nicotiana, 65–6,
Nutmeg, 89

Paprika, 89, 131
Parsley, 31, 72, 131
Patchouli, 45
Pennyroyal, 74
Peony, 55–6, 66,
Pepper, 31
Pheromones, 15, 101
Pine, 45–6,
Pinks/Carnations, 56, 91, 98
Plato, 102
Psychoneuroimmunology, 16

Rose, 25, 46, 62–3, 92–4,
  99–100

Rosemary, 18, 46–7, 72–3
Rosewood, 47,
Rue, 74

St Rosalia of Palermo, 126
St Rose, 126
Saffron, 19, 89–90
Sage, 31, 73
Sandalwood, 23, 26, 47–8, 83
Skin, 37–9, 41–3, 46–8, 51–3
Sleep, 38–9, 44, 51
Smudging, 27–8
Star Anise, 90
Stocks, 66, 82
Stomach, 40, 45,
Stress, 40–1,
Sweet Bay, 69,
Sweet Pea, 66,
Synergy, 36–7

Tansy, 75,
Tarragon, 73
Tea Tree, 36, 48,
Thyme, 28, 73
Turmeric, 90

Vanilla, 90
Violet, 25, 29, 67, 93

Wallflower, 66
Willow, 19, 54, 82
Wine, 96–100
Wisteria, 66–7,

Yarrow, 75,
Ylang-Ylang, 48–9

Zwaardemaker, Hendrick, 102

# *Index*

Agrippa, Henry Cornelius, 127
Allspice, 87
Ambergris, 25, 107
Angelica, 55
Apple, 28,
Astrology, 30, 127–9
Avicenna (Ibn Sina), 31

Bach, Edward, 56–7
Basil, 18, 21, 37, 68–9, 83
Bergamot, 37–8

Caraway, 19, 87
Cardamom, 19, 31, 83, 87
Castor, 107
Cedar, 22–3, 130
Cedarwood, 19, 21–5, 38–9, 83
Chamomile, 19, 38, 74, 83, 95
Chervil, 69,
Chives, 69–70,
Cinnamon, 31, 55, 88
Circulation, 37, 39,
Civet, 107
Clover, 98
Cloves, 31, 55, 83, 88
Colds, 40, 50, 95
Coltsfoot, 98
Coriander, 19, 88
Cowslip, 74, 92
Culpeper, Nicholas, 30,
Cumin, 18, 88
Cypress, 19, 39, 83

Dandelion, 94–5, 98
Dill, 18, 70,
Dioscorides, 55

Elderflower, 91, 95–6, 99, 108–9
Eucalyptus, 39, 83
Evening Primrose, 36,

Fennel, 26, 40,
Fenugreek, 18, 88–9
Frankincense, 19, 21, 40–1, 83
Freesia, 64,

Galen, 55
Gardenia, 64,
Gattefossé, René-Maurice, 30
Geranium, 41,
Ginger, 31, 55, 89
Grapefruit, 10–11, 41–2, 83, 96
Guerlain, House of, 105–6

Hair, 38–9, 47,
Hawthorn, 55,
Hippocrates, 54,
Honeysuckle, 29, 64, 99
Hyssop, 70,

Jasmine, 35, 64, 96
Juniper, 18, 21, 42, 89

Lavender, 26, 42–3, 64, 91
Lemon, 43, 83, 96